Oxfordshire
Edited by Chris Hallam

First published in Great Britain in 2004 by:
Young Writers
Remus House
Coltsfoot Drive
Peterborough
PE2 9JX
Telephone: 01733 890066
Website: www.youngwriters.co.uk

All Rights Reserved

© Copyright Contributors 2004

SB ISBN 1 84460 440 3

Foreword

Young Writers was established in 1991 and has been passionately devoted to the promotion of reading and writing in children and young adults ever since. The quest continues today. Young Writers remains as committed to engendering the fostering of burgeoning poetic and literary talent as ever.

This year's Young Writers competition has proven as vibrant and dynamic as ever and we are delighted to present a showcase of the best poetry from across the UK. Each poem has been carefully selected from a wealth of *Once Upon A Rhyme* entries before ultimately being published in this, our twelfth primary school poetry series.

Once again, we have been supremely impressed by the overall high quality of the entries we have received. The imagination, energy and creativity which has gone into each young writer's entry made choosing the best poems a challenging and often difficult but ultimately hugely rewarding task - the general high standard of the work submitted amply vindicating this opportunity to bring their poetry to a larger appreciative audience.

We sincerely hope you are pleased with our final selection and that you will enjoy *Once Upon A Rhyme Oxfordshire* for many years to come.

Contents

Appleton CE Primary School
Hollie Huggins (11)	1
Christy Nicholson (9)	1
Elliot Bailey (11)	2
Sophie Bell (9)	2
Sam Trinder (11)	3
George Readshaw (10)	3
Alex Cade (9)	3
Gemma Thorpe (10)	4
Jessica-Jane Fox (9)	4
Ashley Bulpitt (9)	5
Lily O'Neill (9)	5
Joanna Chivers (9)	6
Alex Bailey (9)	6
Natalie Wren (9)	6
Claudio Checchia (9)	7
Owen Holloway (9)	7
Robert Dymock (10)	7
Becky Baird (10)	8
Lewis Knox (10)	8
Charlotte-Anne Butler (10)	9
Louise Harrison (10)	9
Robin Smith (10)	9
James Little (11)	10

Bishop Carpenter CE Primary School
Aisha Benfield (7)	10
Matilda Kirwin (8)	11
Jessica Hummer (8)	11
Joseph Howarth (7)	12
Bethanie Simpson (9)	12
Will Barker (9)	13
Charley Harris (8)	13
Louise Hughes (8)	14
Rebecca Wallett (8)	14
William Palmer (8)	15
Emily Jane Eames-Matthews (8)	15
Sophie Davis (7)	16
Ben Davies (8)	16

Drew Venter (9)	17
Jessica Holly Barr (8)	17
Jasmine Theilgaard (9)	17
Rhiannon Khabiri (7)	18
Katie Heritage (7)	18
Ruth Dudfield (8)	18
Eliza Louise Lewis (8)	19
Amy Simpson (7)	19
Tristan Dixon (7)	19
Harry Heathcote (8)	20
Victoria Attridge (7)	20
Katherine Whitmill (8)	21
Bethany Craven (7)	21
Andrew Bridge (8)	21
Rachel Evans (8)	22

Bishop Loveday CE Primary School
Robyn Wilson (8)	22

Brize Norton Primary School
Eleanor Trinder (10)	23
Zoe Calbert (10)	23

Carswell Primary School
Harry Doherty (8)	24
Nicola Louise Kastner (9)	24
Carl Powell (10)	25
Lauren Barnes (7)	25
Karl Harrison (8)	26
Emily Woodville (7)	27
Katie Horsfall (8)	28
Alex Mills (10)	28
Melissa Baker (11)	29
Conor Thomas (9)	29
Amy Dale (7)	30
Lisa Terrie Roberts (10)	30
Craig Connolly (10)	31
Ashleigh Brant (9)	31
Abbie McGaw (9)	32
Macaully Spraggs (10)	32

Jordan Aitken (9)	33
Sebastian Le-Maguet (9)	33
Ryan Harling (10)	34
Martin Johnson (8)	34
James Irving (10)	35
Mason Kelley (10)	35
Steven Dann (10)	36
Michael Ritchie (11)	36
Jade Dianno (10)	37
Laura Johns (10)	37
Rachel Hayden (11)	38
Alice Samways (11)	39
David Otero (11)	39
Harry McCarthy (10)	40
Matthew Gilboy (10)	41
Kirsty Burgoyne (9)	41
Amy Jones (10)	42
Lily Faith Cooper (9)	42
Lois Jamieson (9)	43
Jordan Redford (9)	43
Blain Moorhouse (9)	44
Kelly Fuller (10)	44
Nathan Singh (9)	45
Hannah Greenaway (10)	45
Megan Astley (9)	46
Océane Ufferte (10)	47
Daniel Cross (10)	47
Emily Mullord (10)	48
Emma Thomas (10)	48
Thomas Wilkinson (9)	49
Andrew Vanneck (10)	49
Constant Afun (10)	50
Penny Gray (7)	50
Thomas Mullord (7)	51
Kyle Wilde (9)	51
Joseph Morgan (8)	52
Adi Lusiana Wainiqolo (10)	52
Mitchell Curtis (8)	53
Caroline Church (10)	53
Chloe Frame (8)	54
Emily Cackett (7)	54
Cassidy Sandall (8)	55

Jade Bates (7)	56
Katie Shaw (8)	57
Rebecca Cooper (7)	57
Sarah Greenaway (8)	58
Tamsin Harling (8)	59

Chipping Warden Primary School

Cameron Jon Exeter (9)	59
Thomas Laxton (10)	60
Anna Nash (10)	61
Benjamin Edwards (10)	61
Abbie McCammond (9)	62
Esme Stanley (9)	62
Chloe Cox (9)	63
Sarah Biegel (7)	63
Cassie Forbes (8)	64
Libby Grant (9)	64
Harriet Clarke (9)	65
Lily Waddington (9)	65
Alex Buck (10)	66
Roxanne Clarke (9)	66
Oliver Mason (9)	67
Oliver James Macdonald-Brown (10)	67
Jack Travis Waterhouse (10)	68
Emma Rogers (10)	68
Daniel Spring (9)	69
Sophie Biegel (9)	70

Crowmarsh Gifford Primary School

Patrick Pearce (8)	70
Joshua Bennett (9)	71
Evie Stretch (8)	72
Alexandra Ball (11)	72
Jack Whelan (10)	73
Rebekah Hoodless (10)	73
Daniel Sadler (11)	74
Sammy-Jo Knowles (11)	74
James Kennedy (11)	74
Natasha Jarvis (10)	75
Melissa Whitehouse (10)	75
Thomas Earl (9)	76

Miriam Johnson (10)	76
Chloe Rodwell (11)	77
Emily Diserens (8)	77
Alix Marshall (11)	78
Charlie Phillips (8)	78
Rosie Miller (10)	79
Amy Cherrill (10)	79
Melissa Kalkan (9)	80
Frances Whitehouse (10)	80
Eleanor Chappell (11)	81
Olivia Sherry (10)	81
Ella Bodeker (10)	82
Tahlia Freya Parrett (7)	82
Harry Turner (7)	83

Kirtlington CE Primary School

Bradley Hedges (9)	83
Harriet Owen (10)	84
Douglas Haynes (9)	85
Elliott Sargent (9)	85
Harriet Hunter (9)	86
Patrick Hunter (11)	86
Gareth Preston (10)	87
Zac McEachran & Charlie Brinkworth (9)	88
Josh McEachran (10)	88
Nicole Beahan (10)	89
Megan Bates (9)	90
Rhys Harris (9)	91
Helen Kirby (10)	92
Joe East (8)	93
Alex Rogers (8)	94
Daniella Ashdown (10)	95
Martha Buck Bohan (10)	96

Lynams Dragon Pre-Preparatory School

Felix Frank (8)	96
Molly Tang (8)	97
Ibrahim Ait Tahar (7)	97
Oli Rowlands (7)	98
Alice Dendy (7)	98
Miriam Lawson (7)	99

Flora Cameron Watt (7) 100
Edward Ashcroft (7) 100
Caitlin Lloyd (8) 101
Oliver Faulk (7) 101
Freddy Creed (8) 102
William Bowen (7) 102
Daniel Scott-Kerr (8) 103

Marcham CE Primary School
Kristina Foster (10) 103
Georgia Tolley (10) 103
Kathleen Macnee (11) 104
Georgia Upjohn (11) 104
Rebecca Rowe (9) 105

Marsh Baldon CE Primary School
Rosie Ball (9) 105
Holly Barne (9) 106
Isabel Barne (10) 106
Robyn Brady (11) 107
Laurie Davies (10) 107
Sean Brook (10) 108
Harry Greenaway (10) 108
Alex Gabbidon (9) 109
Holly Williams (10) 110
Emma Stribling (10) 110
Beth Holdforth (10) 111

Moulsford Prep School
Oliver Fogden (11) 111
Freddie Wilcox (10) 112
James Boddie (9) 112
Alasdair Gardiner (10) 112
Alex Bagnall (9) 113
Charlie Beardall (10) 113
Charlie Leslau (10) 114
Richard Leahy (10) 114
Ben Boddington (9) 115
Charles Buchan (10) 115
Sam Rogerson (11) 116

Sandy Pain (9)	117
Louis Williams (9)	117
Felix Newman (10)	118
William Dethridge (9)	119
Auberi Chen (11)	119
Andrew Grant (11)	120
Angus Stephen (9)	121
Edward Hughes (10)	121
Ben Longden (10)	122

Orchard Close, Sibford School

Luke Gartside (10)	122
David Wells (10)	123
Poppy Tibbetts (10)	123
Ellie Shercliff (11)	124
Daniel Pickles (11)	125
Samuel Licence (11)	125
Ishita Bhatnagar	126
Rory McGill (11)	126
Joseph Fallon	127
Deven Pledger (11)	127

Rupert House School

Annie Moberly (10)	128
Augusta Shaida (9)	129
Olivia Knowles (8)	129
Laura Bacon (8)	130
Milly Nunney (8)	130
Jessica Miller (8)	131
Victoria Porter (8)	132
Natalie Jennings (8)	133
Ellen Darke (8)	134
Yasmin Denehy (8)	135
Amy Nicholas (9)	136
Laura Bevan (9)	138
Abigail Leslie (8)	139
Olivia Morris-Soper (9)	140
Jessica Ryan (9)	141
Rebecca Roddan (9)	142
Kate Radin (9)	143
Georgia Chamberlain (8)	144

Chloë Winstanley (8)	145
Katie Adams (9)	146
Emma Ford (10)	147
Sophie Frood (10)	148
India Wishart (8)	149
Lydia Tufnell (8)	150
Katie Moberly (8)	151
Abigail McQuater (9)	152
Harriet Gardner (10)	153

St John's Priory School, Banbury

Jodi Ferguson (10)	153
Georgia Leach (11)	154
Louis Harris (10)	155
Rebecca Smith (10)	155
Thomas Callnon (10)	155
Imogen Webb (10)	156
Sophie Poole (10)	156
Harry Poole (10)	157
Elise Robinson (10)	157
Charlotte Ross (10)	158
Octavia Homans (10)	159
Rachael Lever (8)	159
Alicia Forsyth-Forrest (8)	160
Libby Hart (9)	160
George Walker (10)	161
Hamish Preston (10)	161
Alexandre Dansette (10)	162
Abbie Leach (8)	162
Sarah Williams (9)	163
Hayley Wood (9)	163
Vanessa Wilde (8)	164
James Williams (8)	164
Olivia Attley (8)	165
Isobel Green	165
Thomas Marsden (9)	166
Sooraj Mahesh (8)	166
Kara Watson (8)	167
Fergus Preston (8)	168
Daniel Norrell (9)	168
Benjamin Hawkins (7)	169

Sam Sorabjee (7)   169
Kyle White (8)   170
Vanessa Polson (8)   170
Elizabeth Hurst (8)   170
Akanksha Goyal (7)   171
Rhiannon Gray (8)   171
Moronshayo Oshodi (8)   172
Robert Tibbetts (7)   172
Oliver Walker-Savings (7)   172
Poppy Hawkins (11)   173

Stanford In The Vale Primary School
Daniel Simpson (10)   173
Curtis Redman (10)   174
Max Johnson (11)   174
Craig Punfield (10)   174
Stephanie Jordan (10)   175
Danielle Belcher (10)   175
Lauren Pilcher (10)   176
Harriet Munday (10)   176
Josh Satchell (11)   177
Amber Gifford (11)   177
Rachel Hanna (10)   178
Gemma New (11)   178
Philip Johnson (11)   179
Rozanna Harrison (10)   179
Callum Eynstone (11)   180
Sid Ashley (10)   180
Kay Leighfield (11)   181
Rebecca Kent (10)   181
Graham Edgecombe (11)   182
Bill Fraser (10)   182
Sherrie Drew (10)   183

The Poems

Playground Personification

The air kicked the gutters as they gurgled and
Chattered to each other.

The nocturnal lamp posts unbolted their dazzling eyes
As the twilight strolled over the hills to welcome them.

The old icy gate tried to act casual
As impostors invaded its grounds.

The ancient Biffa bin yawned as it awoke from a long, deep sleep,
Ready to be fed breakfast from the cleaners, but five minutes later
                                              it's empty inside.

Hollie Huggins (11)
Appleton CE Primary School

Haiku

Black and white I am,
I live in the Antarctic,
I hate polar bears.

I am a penguin.

Standing high it is,
Rocky paths lead all the way
Highest peak snow-capped.

I am a mountain.

Round like a football
Ticking just like a heartbeat,
Attached to your hand.

I am a watch.

Christy Nicholson (9)
Appleton CE Primary School

Time For School

People running, they're late again,
Teachers saying, 'Where's my pen?'

The board is filled with useless writing,
Out the window, toddlers fighting.

Everybody's in the room,
Cleaners cleaning with a broom.

'Teacher, please Sir, show me how,'
Ooh! Time for break, I'm going now.

Elliot Bailey (11)
Appleton CE Primary School

The Deep Dark Night

It was so dark
That the shimmering
Stars wouldn't shine.

It was so silent
That I could hear
The moon go by.

It was so clear
That I could see
The rain snuggled in
The fluffy clouds.

Sophie Bell (9)
Appleton CE Primary School

Animals

The peaceful deer lies comfortably on the ground,
Munching on the grass.

8,400 miles away, the lightning-fast cheetah is running across Africa,
Chasing gazelles as it goes.

The painfully-slow tortoise is crawling through the long grass
At approximately 0 mph.

The deer is drifting through the moonlit field
Still munching on the grass.

Sam Trinder (11)
Appleton CE Primary School

In The Playground

In the playground the trees stretch
And the grass waves.

The bin groans for its breakfast
And the gate moans 'shut me up!'

The goal net is hurried along by the wind
And the bench waits and waits.

But the wall stays blank
In the playground.

George Readshaw (10)
Appleton CE Primary School

Haiku Fish

See the shiny scales
Darting past like a rocket
Colourful and bright.

Alex Cade (9)
Appleton CE Primary School

The Playground

The old bell rang and children rushed out to play
The old crumpled gate faints on passers-by in the dull weather
The broken bench moans in the dark corner as people pass by
The dirty Biffa bin groans as litter invades it
The cracked wall shudders as children bash it
The dusty wood chipping struggle as children crush them
The old bell rang and children walked into school.

Gemma Thorpe (10)
Appleton CE Primary School

Black Cat Alphabet

A black cat
delicately eats
fresh grubs
hungrily
interested in
juicy kippers
longing to
munch nothing
other than
perfect quails
rabbit salmon
or tuna under
the veranda
then when
'xhausted he
yawns and
zzzzzleeps.

Jessica-Jane Fox (9)
Appleton CE Primary School

When I Feed My Rabbit

When I feed my rabbit
I always do the same
I lift up the cage lid
And call out his name.

When I feed my rabbit
He cautiously creeps up to me
He loves salty water
So I get it from the sea.

When I feed my rabbit
I put in some hay
I put in some fresh food
And it's all gone in a day.

When I feed my rabbit
I lay down some straw
Trouble is he eats it up
So I put out some more.

When I feed my rabbit
The moon gets very deep
And when I look down at him
He is fast asleep.

Ashley Bulpitt (9)
Appleton CE Primary School

Mountains Haiku

Many metres high
rising over everything
making huge hills small.

Lily O'Neill (9)
Appleton CE Primary School

House

The chimney coughed and took a breath of fresh air.
The roof shivered as the wind blew.
The windows yawned as they got opened day in and day out,
The door clapped as it was slammed shut.
The walls groaned as the football was kicked at them.

Joanna Chivers (9)
Appleton CE Primary School

Snake

Slimy slithering creature,
Climbing trees over the ground through the seas
Bang goes the jaws
Slash goes the claws
The object's prey fades away
Never to see the day again.

Alex Bailey (9)
Appleton CE Primary School

Darkness

Darkest forces come together,
You will rule forever and ever.

If the light struggles through,
I will consider beating you.

All the orcs will collide,
Maybe do a suicide.

Ha ha, we won,
Light, ha ha, is gone.

Natalie Wren (9)
Appleton CE Primary School

Magic Forest

In the magic forest
There are birds, mysterious birds.

In the magic forest
There are dragons, barbaric dragons.

In the magic forest
There are penguins, iced penguins.

In the magic forest
There are winds, furious winds.

Claudio Checchia (9)
Appleton CE Primary School

Living Playground

The spotless windows smile in the bright sun.
The bark, as hard as rock regularly falling off the moaning tree.
The bin breathes fresh air again. As rubbish flies out of its mouth.
The old wooden gate groans as children kick a ball against it.

Owen Holloway (9)
Appleton CE Primary School

Thought

They are big
They are tall
They are amazing at maths
And good at art
They have a brilliant imagination
They thought up our household items . . .
An inventor!

Robert Dymock (10)
Appleton CE Primary School

The Forest

Deep in the forest,
Strange things are about to happen.

As the scattering mice find a house to sleep in,
Strange things are about to happen.

Out comes a witch with her wand and her broom,
Strange things are about to happen.

She says the wrong spell, 'Oh no, what a shame!'
Strange things are about to happen.

The trees sigh gently as the wind blows.
The grass walks as slow as a slug now

Because strange things have happened.

Becky Baird (10)
Appleton CE Primary School

The Mad World

The shaven head of the fir tree
Stands tall above the ground
Wailing as he gets hot

The uneven peaks of the mountain
Bellow as the
Mountaineers ascend them

The fiery mouth of the volcano
Hisses with sickness
As the hot lava comes rushing out

The bawling of the lonely yeti
Rings throughout the mountain range
For all the yaks to hear

The swerving water in the river
Collides with the banks
All the way to the sea.

Lewis Knox (10)
Appleton CE Primary School

The Girl's Cloakroom

The fire bell groaned as it sprang into action,
The toilets moaned as a hand made them tremble.
The pegs jumped as a girl dropped her bag and left,
The floor cried as people stepped on it.
The benches laughed as someone sat on them.

Charlotte-Anne Butler (10)
Appleton CE Primary School

Woods

In the cursed winter woods,
Trees whisper to each other,
Their round hypnotic eyes open
As they take their first step into sunlight.

Louise Harrison (10)
Appleton CE Primary School

Tanka

Swinging vine to vine
Hairy belly sticking out
Arms so flexible
Acrobating through the trees
Never slowing down to breathe

'Ooh, ooh!' he's yelling
With words you don't really know
His rival, the chimp
Hungrily searching for him
But he's hidden away.

I am a monkey.

Robin Smith (10)
Appleton CE Primary School

City Jungle

The tired trees stretch their stiff backs
As the new day begins.

As the ferocious wind rages, the leaves
Tumble and trip and the rain
Pounces like a lion.

Then the children come, laughing and playing,
Chattering and running, as though
They were monkeys.

And the long black snake
Swallows the mice
Which run along its back.

Then, as the mountainous houses
Loom in the mist,
Parrot paragliders swoop and dive
With their colourful feathers
And human speech,

And the big elephant buses
Roam across the country
With monkey humans riding them.

But then we wake up and realise
It's just a dream,
A dream, a dream, a dream.

James Little (11)
Appleton CE Primary School

Seasons

Spring is a wake-up from a big sleep
Summer is when the flowers peep,
Autumn is when leaves are in their heaps,
Winter is quiet and nothing leaps.

Aisha Benfield (7)
Bishop Carpenter CE Primary School

Cats

The curtains draw back
The music starts
The crowd roars
People cheer
Lights come up
As Rum Tum Tugger opens the show

Magical Macavity leaps through the air
Drums beat hard
He cuts the power
All is dark
Shhhh!
Quiet!
Cats run off stage
Day comes up, Macavity is gone
Chief comes on . . .
It's Macavity!

Rum Tum Tugger starts to sing
As Mungojerrie and Rumpelteazer dance around
The show ends
T S Elliot's Cats are a success once more
The crowd all roar!

Matilda Kirwin (8)
Bishop Carpenter CE Primary School

Winter

W inter is here
I cicles hang from the roof
N orth Pole weather
T rees are bare
E veryone wraps up warm
R ain is falling down.

Jessica Hummer (8)
Bishop Carpenter CE Primary School

Spring

S pringing daffodils shine so bright
P eople smell them with delight.
R ain and sun make a lovely rainbow
I ndigo and orange colours that flow into
N ice flowers which
G racefully grow.

Joseph Howarth (7)
Bishop Carpenter CE Primary School

Seasons

The summer is scorching hot
but I like it ever such a lot!
The birds are twittering and cheeping
lambs are skipping and leaping.

Autumn is the time leaves fall -
this is the time we celebrate harvest festival.
Leaves jump off the trees to hide,
whilst children enjoy playing outside.

Snowdrops fall from the sky
animals hibernate - we all know why!
Children make angels in the snow
'Don't throw that snowball!'
'Whoa!'

Spring is a lovely wake-up call with flowers everywhere
look in your garden, I think you will find lots there!
Leaves return on trees
animals venture out including bumblebees.

Bethanie Simpson (9)
Bishop Carpenter CE Primary School

Meat

Chicken, chicken, lovely chicken
This is where the gravy's stickin'
Sausage sizzling in the pan
Pull it out and it'll have a tan.

I think the best meat must be lamb
It beats turkey and it beats ham
I just really, really hate salami
I'd much prefer origami.

Bacon's what I like to cook
Though I have to be careful of the bacon crook
Mince is what I've always feared
And when I say that, I get jeered.

Will Barker (9)
Bishop Carpenter CE Primary School

The Soft White Snow

The soft white snow
The soft white snow
Falls down from the sky.

The soft white snow
The soft white snow
Twinkling in the sky.

The soft white snow
The soft white snow
Lights up the sky.

The soft white snow
The soft white snow
As peaceful as you and I.

Charley Harris (8)
Bishop Carpenter CE Primary School

Late For Class

'You're late!' said Miss.
'The bell has gone,
Dinner numbers done
And work begun.
What have you got to say for yourself?'

'Well it's like this Miss
Me sister was sick,
Me dog fell down the stairs,
The wheel came off me bike
And then we lost our Robyn's snake.
Ear ache struck me dad,
And me aunt had quite a funny turn.'

'Yes, yes, now get on with your work, quickly!'

'But please Miss, I don't know what to do!'

Louise Hughes (8)
Bishop Carpenter CE Primary School

Will Young

Will Young, pop idol
Fans cheer for him
Crowds of people came to see him
Sing his number one song

Will Young, pop idol
Earns millions of pounds
For a record deal
Will Young, pop idol
Will always lights my fire!

Rebecca Wallett (8)
Bishop Carpenter CE Primary School

Michael Schumacher

M ichael Schumacher
I s ready for a race.
C oming to win,
H e is the very best.
A ppeals every race,
E very race he wins
L oving a victory.

S ee, he's very fast,
C an't catch him.
H e's just too fast.
U nless you are as fast as a car,
M ichael will beat you
A lso loves being a champion
C atch him if you can
H e is the fastest man.
E at his dust,
R acing is his career.

William Palmer (8)
Bishop Carpenter CE Primary School

Seasons

S un springs up in the sunny air,
E agles swarm around in the sky.
A nimals are playing, lambs are leaping,
S easons are hot, cold and warm.
O ranges are delicious and juicy in summertime
N ovember is a chilly month,
S un shines in summer.

Emily Jane Eames-Matthews (8)
Bishop Carpenter CE Primary School

Spring

Spring is so cool,
I see baby foals and lambs,
Chicks and birds,
All the birds sing a happy song.

Spring is fun,
Easter comes and children run.
Spring is calm all day long.
I see sheep, I love to feed them.
Spring is nice.
The sun is as gold as a conker.

Sophie Davis (7)
Bishop Carpenter CE Primary School

Owl

Wise
Nocturnal
Magnificent owl
Swooping to the trees
Silently
Hungrily
Like a pair of binoculars
I would not like you in a cage
Owl, wise owl.

Ben Davies (8)
Bishop Carpenter CE Primary School

Sausages

Pork sausages, pork sausages,
You're so hot, you sizzle in the pot.
When I eat you, you're so lovely,
I want you every night.

Spicy sausages, spicy sausages,
You're so hot you burn my mouth, every time.
I scream when I try
I will never ever try you again.

Drew Venter (9)
Bishop Carpenter CE Primary School

My Puppy Lolly

A sheet of black
Jumping high, plays all day
Sleeps all night, soft as silk
Running free.
Run, run yippee!
Lights go out, she's tired out.
No more shouts, curled up on a bed of fleece.

Jessica Holly Barr (8)
Bishop Carpenter CE Primary School

Spring

S pring arrives, leaving the dark winter long behind
P eeping buds waiting to explode into a rainbow of colours,
R ays of dappled sunlight peering through the sleepy trees,
I cy stems transform into early morning dew,
N ewborn lambs skip and play, accepting the world around them
G ardens embracing all of nature for the new beginning.

Jasmine Theilgaard (9)
Bishop Carpenter CE Primary School

Winter

W inter wind blows from the north.
I cicles go drip, drip, drip on the ground
N orth Pole weather is here
T rees are covered in snow
E veryone is wrapping up warm
R ain is falling into puddles.

Rhiannon Khabiri (7)
Bishop Carpenter CE Primary School

Autumn Leaves

Autumn leaves fall off the trees,
Children are dancing in the breeze.
Trees sway in the cool blow,
Waiting patiently for frost and snow.

Katie Heritage (7)
Bishop Carpenter CE Primary School

The Horse

Noble
Proud
Strong
Horse
Swift as the wind
Powerful
Graceful
Brave as a lion
They mean the world to me
The horse
Noble horse.

Ruth Dudfield (8)
Bishop Carpenter CE Primary School

Steve Irwin

S teve Irwin, a nature guy
T rapping and saving crocs.
E arning praise from everyone
V ery brave in all he does,
E ntertaining kids and crocs alike on TV.

I . . .
R eally like his shows,
W ell done Steve!
I t really thrills me
N ow I am your biggest fan.

Eliza Louise Lewis (8)
Bishop Carpenter CE Primary School

Rabbits

I have several furry little rabbits
My rabbits all have lots of funny habits
My rabbits are very, very cute
They enjoy nibbling treats like fruit
My rabbits run around their hutches
I like watching them very much
Sometimes they gnaw
Very near to their door.

Amy Simpson (7)
Bishop Carpenter CE Primary School

Ronaldo

Ronaldo runs so fast
His boots glow in the dark
He runs faster than a speeding bullet
He is so good when he scores . . .
Everyone shouts!

Tristan Dixon (7)
Bishop Carpenter CE Primary School

Africa

A pes jump by the horizon
F iery sun hotter than an oven
R attle snakes slivering and sliding
I ndigo sky, yellow hornbill flies by
C rocodile snatches the meat
A frican ants scurry along the floor.

Harry Heathcote (8)
Bishop Carpenter CE Primary School

Seasons

Spring is a wake-up
Baby animals are born
All flowers bloom.

Summer, summer shining, summer
Bumblebees buzzing
Days become longer, nights become shorter.

Beautiful autumn
All of the leaves are falling
Parks are deserted
Autumn winds howl around my ears.

Winter is cold, windy and snowy
Christmas warmth is around the corner
Everyone enjoying festivals indoors
Spring is on its way back.

Victoria Attridge (7)
Bishop Carpenter CE Primary School

Spaghetti

Spaghetti whirling around my fork,
Yum yum,
It's like slimy worms wriggling into my mouth.
It's even better with meatballs.
Sometimes it's very messy,
It's like little squiggly lines.
I love meatballs and spaghetti.
Come on buy some right now, you might like them too.
It makes me scared when I put them in my mouth.

Katherine Whitmill (8)
Bishop Carpenter CE Primary School

Spring

Shining sun wakes up
People taking their coats off for the first time
Rabbits having babies in the fields
Now the flowers are growing in the field
Going to the seaside.

Bethany Craven (7)
Bishop Carpenter CE Primary School

Football

F ootballers jog on the pitch
O wen's for Liverpool - ready for the match
O wen passes to Gerrard, the match starts,
T his is Owen's first match of the FA Cup
B rilliant ball control by Gerrard
A ll the supporters are yelling, 'Shoot!'
L iverpool scores - victory is Liverpool's
L oud as loud can be the crowd cheers. Liverpool wins!

Andrew Bridge (8)
Bishop Carpenter CE Primary School

Snow At School

It's not fair
It's just not fair,
I have to go to school.

It's not fair,
It's just not fair,
I've got work to do.

It's not fair,
It's just not fair,
I don't get to play.

It's not fair,
It's just not fair,
I wish it were home time.

Rachel Evans (8)
Bishop Carpenter CE Primary School

Rainbow

R ainbows are all different colours
A pple green, fluorescent blue, rich brown, a super scarlet
I ndigo and a pretty pink
N o one will ever find the pot of gold
B ecause you are too far away from the goodness that lies at the end
O nce you find yourself in peace, you will find the pot of gold.
W ill you ever find the goodness which lies at the end of the rainbow?

Robyn Wilson (8)
Bishop Loveday CE Primary School

Summer

On summer days,
My dog plays,
With his yellow tennis ball
And then he stops to look at the trees so tall
And the apple that is about to fall.

On summer days,
My mum says,
'Would you like an ice cream
From the ice cream van?'
While she was lying and getting a tan.

On summer days
My brother says,
'When are these hot summer days gonna be over?
They are very hot days.'

Eleanor Trinder (10)
Brize Norton Primary School

Winter

It's so cold, cold, cold,
The wind is bold, bold, bold
The rain is wet, wet, wet.

We splash in the puddles with wet socks
With a warm coat wrapped around us.
It is winter.

Zoe Calbert (10)
Brize Norton Primary School

The School Sound Collector
(Based on 'The Sound Collector' by Roger McGough)

A stranger called this morning
Dressed all in black and grey,
Put all the sounds into a bag
And took them all away.

The shouting of the children,
The rustling of the trees.
The clattering of the equipment,
The buzzing of the bees.

The dripping of the tap,
The slurping of the drink.
The munching of the food,
The gurgling of the sink.

A stranger called this morning,
He didn't leave his name.
Left us only silence,
Life will never be the same.

Harry Doherty (8)
Carswell Primary School

Peace

Peace is as white as a dove,
Peace smells like fresh air in the open,
Peace tastes like clean, cold water,
Peace sounds like water lashing at the sand,
Peace feels like cotton wool,
Peace lives in the world.

Nicola Louise Kastner (9)
Carswell Primary School

D-Day

Bullets firing far and near,
Hearing the metal penetrating.
Our soldiers filled with fear.
Closing in on the border is frightening
Men falling into the water.
War is hard but exciting.
We are on the borders of France
Not all have made it this far -
But we got this far, so we must advance.

Carl Powell (10)
Carswell Primary School

In The Farm

Down on the farm
Down on the farm
Horses go neigh
Horses go *neigh!*

Down on the farm
Down on the farm
Pigs go oink
Pigs go *oink!*

Down on the farm
Down on the farm
Sheep go baa
Sheep go *baa!*

Down on the farm
Down on the farm
Cows go moo
Cows go *moo!*

Lauren Barnes (7)
Carswell Primary School

The Weather

What is the weather?
What is the weather?
It is raining
It is raining!

What is the weather?
What is the weather?
It is sunny
It is sunny!

What is the weather?
What is the weather?
It is windy
It is windy!

What is the weather
What is the weather?
It is thundering
It is thundering!

What is the weather?
What is the weather?
It is lightning
It is lightning!

Karl Harrison (8)
Carswell Primary School

Down In The Ocean

Down in the ocean
Down in the ocean
Jellyfish go squish
Jellyfish go *squish!*

Down in the ocean
Down in the ocean
Dolphins go eek
Dolphins go *eek!*

Down in the ocean
Down in the ocean
Lobsters go clip
Lobsters go *clip!*

Down in the ocean
Down in the ocean
Sharks go snap
Sharks go *snap!*

Down in the ocean
Down in the ocean
Swim for your life
Swim for your life!

Emily Woodville (7)
Carswell Primary School

In The Farm

Down on the farm
Down on the farm
Horses go neigh
Horses go *neigh!*

Down on the farm
Down on the farm
Pigs go oink
Pigs go *oink!*

Down on the farm
Down on the farm
Sheep go baa
Sheep go *baa!*

Down on the farm
Down on the farm
Run for your life
Run for your life!

Katie Horsfall (8)
Carswell Primary School

Rugby

E xciting
N early beaten by Australia
G reat!
L ook mean
A mazing!
N obody can beat them.
D on't mess with them!

Alex Mills (10)
Carswell Primary School

Valentine's Day

Valentine's Day is all about love
Like a Guardian Angel from up above
There's flowers, chocolates - but mostly roses.
All about husbands and wives
Together, spending time
And always saying to each other,
'You're forever mine!'
Your husband will buy you something nice
Or take you out for a meal
And tell you how they feel.

Melissa Baker (11)
Carswell Primary School

On The Farm

Down on the farm
Down on the farm
Pigs to oink, oink
Pigs go *oink, oink!*

Down on the farm
Down on the farm
Dogs go woof woof
Dogs go *woof woof!*

Down on the farm
Down on the farm,
Ducks go quack quack
Ducks go *quack quack!*

Run for your life
Run for your *life!*

Conor Thomas (9)
Carswell Primary School

What Is The Weather?

What is the weather?
What is the weather?
The weather is sunny
The weather is sunny

What is the weather?
What is the weather?
The weather is lightning
The weather is lightning

What is the weather?
What is the weather?
The weather is raining
The weather is raining

What is the weather?
What is the weather?
The weather is windy
The weather is windy.

Amy Dale (7)
Carswell Primary School

My Family

I love my family,
They are so cool.
We all live happily,
They get me out of school.
My sister is now five,
There is something about her
She sometimes lies.
But that doesn't stop me from loving her
That is the same with the rest.

Lisa Terrie Roberts (10)
Carswell Primary School

Fishing Is Cool

F ishing is cool
I like going fishing with my dad
S tarting early in the morning, finishing late at night,
H aving fun all day long,
I caught my biggest fish at Radley
N ow I go there all the time,
G agging to catch a bigger fish all day long.

Craig Connolly (10)
Carswell Primary School

Dolphins Of The Deep Blue

D olphins are delicate
O bviously very intelligent
L ook at dolphins curl
P erhaps you might see them twirl
H ave a glimpse and try to see the king
I have. Have you ever heard them sing?
N ice and soft they hover over the water
S ofter and softer, they go under water.

O ver they jump and splash
F lashing in the sun

T hey wouldn't hurt a fly
H ear them talk as they have loads of fun
E ven the sun won't stop them on their journey

D eeper and deeper they swam
E ager and terrified but they still keep going
E ven a shark won't stop them
P eeping at the sun but don't lose their concentration.

B lue sea shines so bright
L ooking ahead and seeing the light
U sing only love to fill their hearts
E ven if they die, their love won't.

Ashleigh Brant (9)
Carswell Primary School

My Family

My family is the best
Better than the rest
First is my mum
If she eats toast
She will never leave a crumb
Second is my dad
When I'm naughty
He gets very mad.
Next is my sister
Who is very, very bright
And she shines like a light
Last is me, as quiet as a mouse
when it's bingo night
I like to shout, 'House!'

Abbie McGaw (9)
Carswell Primary School

Hallowe'en

Sun down, moon up,
The night of fright was here.
On Hallowe'en the ghosts will play,
Their daily game of fear.

As the ghosts roam the town,
The kids all run and hide.
Then the ghosts will come,
And keep them hostage inside.

Macaully Spraggs (10)
Carswell Primary School

Spiders

Spiders, spiders looking in my eyes
They are eating very healthy flies.
Spiders, spiders still looking in my eyes
With a dozen eyes.
Spider, spider, please go away!
You're too scary for me and
Also too hairy!
Run, run away and never come back,
Go to your family and have a nice nap.
Please don't go inside you will frighten my mum
Now she's on the run!
Spider, spider, where do you put your flies?
Oh that's where - in your belly
Just like on the telly!
Spider, spider, please go away
Or you will get put away.
Off he goes, down the road,
Begging for clothes.

Jordan Aitken (9)
Carswell Primary School

The Secret Changer

It lives beneath a heavy stone
It'll eat and eat until you're bone.

It lives for ever and always sleeps
It waits for the moment and then it leaps.

Its life is weakened with every lie
And the person who finds him
Will eventually die!

Sebastian Le-Maguet (9)
Carswell Primary School

The White Hound

The white hound comes when it snows
You can't hear him when the wind blows
You can't see his teeth, you don't want to know,
The white hound doesn't make a sound,
I'll give you a pound until he's found.

I ran to the woods, I've found him
But he ran without a sound,
This place is out of bounds!

Ryan Harling (10)
Carswell Primary School

Spiders

Spiders, spiders are so scary
Very black and very hairy.
Creeping around
Not making a sound
Eating flies
Looking straight at my eyes
Eating insects, wrapping up flies
Still look straight at my eyes.
Spiders have got eyes to see
The healthy flies.
Spiders have got eight legs to move fast
Even though they look slow,
A spider is hairy and very, very scary.
Spiders are smelly and they have a big belly
And they watch the telly.

Martin Johnson (8)
Carswell Primary School

Chaos Space Marines

Chaos space marines are vile, evil soldiers that reign terror
                                          amongst the Earth,
For they are destroyers of peace, love, joy, happiness and mirth.
They are the enemies of space marines, but they fear their wrath.
But when they defeat and capture the space marines they laugh.
The chaos space marines were once space marines themselves,
But they were turned into chaos space marines by hate and torture.

James Irving (10)
Carswell Primary School

Arsenal Scores Again

Every time I see Arsenal play
Almost every Saturday
They score a goal, always win
They shove the other team right in the bin.
Of course you can see, they're my favourite team
They're big nasty, strong and mean
They've been my favourite since I can remember
Six years ago in September.
They're rarely beaten, they're too good
When we score, they cheer as they're stood.
If you beat them, you've got some skill
Go Arsenal, Kill, Kill, Kill!
Everybody thinks Man Utd is the best
But they know Arsenal better
Than all the rest.
I really, really, can't wait again
When Arsenal wins, they scored zero, we scored ten!

Mason Kelley (10)
Carswell Primary School

The Greatest Match Ever

It's Real Madrid vs Man Utd
The entire crowd is going *Boo!*
It's the beginning of the match
The first shot was taken by Real but I forgot
That the keeper couldn't catch!
It's 2-0 to Man Utd
But I noticed that Luis Figo was short-sighted.
They're playing their best players,
If we win, they will have to pay us.
It's half-time and things are going fine -
But Beckham meets up with Posh
And started to drink wine!

Steven Dann (10)
Carswell Primary School

Dark Elder

The Dark Elder mutant's horror lies in all that
see them, torture is worse than death itself.
Humans mutated, infested, killed in research,
led by a man who is now a beast called Unkuracker,
who was known as King Kelltros.

The space marine's call of the Emperor, you cannot fear them
for they are fear itself.
Hell-bound for they are soon to be like the Dark Elder, mutated,
killed in research, they can't be killed for they're already dead.
So pray they *don't take you alive!*

Michael Ritchie (11)
Carswell Primary School

My Pet Dog

My pet dog is furry and sweet,
Her favourite thing is to eat meat.
She loves jumping in the lake,
And she gets really dirty, for goodness sake.
She has long brown, nice little hair.
To be honest she's just like a cuddly bear,
She loves jumping and running all day long
And to make her sleep you sing her a song.
She's always happy to see you when you enter the door,
When you stroke her fur she wants more, more, more.
She never bites or even hurts you,
Even though she's only two.
She wags her tail with a smile on her face,
And in my heart she's really *Ace!*

Jade Dianno (10)
Carswell Primary School

I Love Max

I love Max

L ovely and cuddly,
O f course he is,
V ery hyper he can be,
E very minute of every hour of every day.

M axy he is called,
A nd of course, he's a German Shepherd,
X mas was fun for my dog and guess what?
　　　　I love Max.

Laura Johns (10)
Carswell Primary School

The Last Unicorn

When the wind's a torrent of darkness,
And the sky's a cloudy grey.
When the creatures are a-hiding,
There they will stay.
When she's seen in the forest
Though she may be old and worn,
They will gasp at the sight of her
At the last unicorn.
When the dragons are a-warning,
All of the fish in the sea,
Shall wait till the morning
Is it to be?
She's the horse with the purity,
The horse with the horn,
Trying to seek a friend,
Is the last unicorn.
I'm alive! I'm alive!
If her horn touches water,
All health is in the horn.
When they stare in the forest
At the last unicorn.
When they look into the sky we're through,
Though she may be old and worn,
They will stare unbelieving -
It's the last unicorn,
I'm alive! I'm alive!

Rachel Hayden (11)
Carswell Primary School

Posh Ladies

Stringy stockings and clean white gloves
Long expensive dresses and glossy doves
Long hair, tied back neatly in a bun
Umbrellas when raining and thimble on thumb
Living in mansions with 2.4 children
Married to someone quite posh and quite fit
Drinking with their finger, stuck out in the sky
(This is so silly, so why do it! Why?)
Talking with their 'T's and 'D's
Sitting with one hand perched on knee . . .
Yuck!
I prefer to be a normal child
Speaking in slang - which they never did!
When I am old or at least grown-up
I'll never get snooty or stuck-up
I'll eat pizza until I'm full
Then I'll rush to the pub and drink Red Bull!

Alice Samways (11)
Carswell Primary School

Snowy Poem

Snow, snow is a wonderful thing,
It comes in winter but never in spring.

It's fun for making snowballs,
But we'll go back inside when my mum calls.

Now I end this poem, with something very nice,
I'll wait until the snow comes sometime next year
When the snow comes in the morning, I give a little cheer.

David Otero (11)
Carswell Primary School

Pure Ambition

I'd like to be a lawyer
And wear a wig in court,
And I'd love my pay cheque
To end in seven noughts.

I'd like to wear a black gown,
And stand up in the dock,
Giving prosecutions only
And making the jury shiver in their socks.

I'd shout, *'Guilty! Guilty! Guilty!'*
And make the prisoners quake.
I'll make guards so frightened,
And never call a break.

There is no telling what I could do,
In my gown of black,
And at the defending lawyer,
I'll aim a hefty *whack!*

The toughest, roughest robbers,
For mummy they would scream,
The sight of my ferocious frown,
Would blast them to smithereens.

No wait, my wig's not big enough,
I want to turn 'em all to fudge,
In fact, a lawyer's not for me . . .
I want to be a *judge!*

Harry McCarthy (10)
Carswell Primary School

Feet

Some feet smell of cheese
And some have fleas,
Some don't like the sea
And some say, please -
'Take your socks off, we can't breathe!'

Some feet are fat and flat
And some are small and round,
Some are fat and chubby
And some are bony and skinny.

Some are hairy like monkeys,
Some bald like a baby's bum,
Some are ugly and you can't look at them
And some are pretty because of nail varnish.

Matthew Gilboy (10)
Carswell Primary School

Flowers

Flowers are all different colours,
Red, yellow, pink and purple.
They smell like a petal falling off a flower,
They are soft and spiky
All flowers are sticky and wet
Some flowers are furry
Most flowers are very pretty
Some are big, some are small
Flowers are very colourful
Most people love them
All flowers are different
And all flowers are special.

Kirsty Burgoyne (9)
Carswell Primary School

Under The Bed

There's a monster under my bed,
But I never dare to look,
Or he'll bring up his scaly hand
And I'll be gone for good!

There's a monster under my bed,
Oh, please leave me alone!
I'm starting to get frightened here,
I'm turning to skin and bone!

There's a monster under my bed,
I saw him pack his suitcase,
I wonder what's he's doing
And why he's got my shoelace?

The monster's gone,
The monster's gone,
Hip, hip, hip, hooray!
But I just heard
A growling, oh, please not today!

Amy Jones (10)
Carswell Primary School

As Red As . . .

Blood from the victims of a sunken ship,
Devils killing humans, screaming at their nip,
Mars in the sky all night,
Sun shining ever so bright,
Flames flickering brightly,
Holly berries ripening lightly,
Poppies swaying in the breeze,
Red hair blowing and making me sneeze.

Lily Faith Cooper (9)
Carswell Primary School

My Brother Is . . .

My brother is special,
He has curly hair,
He dances to music,
And he doesn't like to share.

My brother is sweet,
He likes to play with wires,
He screams in the night,
And makes me really tired.

My brother is cute,
He loves to have a cuddle,
He gets to sleep,
By having a snuggle.

Lois Jamieson (9)
Carswell Primary School

Fireworks

Firework, firework,
Smashing in the sky,
They look like
Flames up above,
A coloured rainbow
Crackling in the air.

Bonfire crackling
And crumbling,
Below the sky,
It smells like smoke
From a fire.

Jordan Redford (9)
Carswell Primary School

Cheetahs

Cheetah's skin is as yellow as the sun,
With polka dots like small dark portals,
Their teeth are like pointy icicles,
Their claws are like little knives,
Their pointy ears are like big mountains,
When they run it looks like they are flying,
They run like the speed of light,
Their cubs are small and cuddly,
Two months later, faster and faster,
They join the hunt.

Blain Moorhouse (9)
Carswell Primary School

My Family

My mum is fun,
She's a great mother,
She is just so caring,
She buys me everything I want.

My dad won't rest,
He's just into music,
Sometimes I'm sick of music,
My dad can shout,
But not as loud as me.

My brother, he is sweet,
He makes me feel a part of the family,
I shout at him
But I really regret it.

My family is so perfect,
The best family in the universe,
But then again, I might be dreaming.

Kelly Fuller (10)
Carswell Primary School

The World

The world is good,
The world is bad,
The world is funny,
The world is sad,
And we are living on it,
So glad, so very glad.

People are black,
People are white,
People are bad,
People are good,
And I know you're very sad.

Nathan Singh (9)
Carswell Primary School

My Family

My mum she cleans,
To make things gleam,
The tables are better,
When the days get wetter.

My dad helps around,
While he makes a lot of sound,
He can always be found,
Carrying more than a pound.

My sister likes to play,
Till she gets her own way,
She likes to eat peas
And play along with me.

And there's me who likes to read,
And many more others,
There's aunties and uncles,
Two sisters and one brother.

Hannah Greenaway (10)
Carswell Primary School

The Seaside

As I walk along the sand,
I've got my bucket and spade in my hand,
'We're going to the seaside,' I shout out loud,
I'm happy, cheerful and very proud,
I'm sweating, it's a really hot day,
'Please can I have a cold drink Mum?' I say.
After that I go in the sea,
Oh no there's a big wave,
Which went all over the people who were trying to sunbathe,
I filled my bucket with the water,
Oh what's this? Here comes a reporter,
Bad idea, you shouldn't have come today,
'Coming through, watch out,' I say,
Once I got very close, do you know what I did?
I threw it all over his clothes,
I got into trouble, of course,
And we had to go home,
When we got there, I kicked the garden gnome,
He fell over and broke into pieces,
I had to go up to my room,
Because I told my mum she looked like a baboon,
That was my day over,
Maybe I'll be able to do it again some day,
Nobody knows but for now, I have to stay in Summer Bay.

Megan Astley (9)
Carswell Primary School

Face

I am a girl,
The girls have long or short hair,
We can have different coloured hair,
It can be black, brown or blonde,
They can have curly hair or straight hair,
We can have different eyes,
We can have blue eyes, brown eyes or green eyes.

We can have Chinese eyes or other eyes,
We can have sunglasses or reading glasses,
We can have big lips or small lips,
We can have a big nose or a small nose
We can have different shaped ears,
We can have earrings and nose rings,
We can have fine eyebrows or big eyebrows.

The boys have the same face
But they haven't got long hair.

Océane Ufferte (10)
Carswell Primary School

Willow Pattern Poem

Two doves flying in the sky,
Up where the clouds float by.

Willow tree standing tall and high,
Up to the place where the birds fly.

Little boat passing by,
Underneath the deep blue sky.

Palace standing tall and strong,
To the bell that goes ding, dong, dong.

And the pattern that never ends,
To the fence that bends.

Daniel Cross (10)
Carswell Primary School

My Cat Kitty

My cat Kitty,
She would love to roam the city,
But I wouldn't let her,
All the car fumes could ruin her fur.

At four o'clock she comes down for tea,
Kitty comes to see me,
For me to get her food,
She always is in a good mood after her food.

Emily Mullord (10)
Carswell Primary School

Valentine Poem

Birds are singing
Bells are ringing,
Valentine's Day is here again,
How many cards have you got?
You've got about ten!

How many love letters have you got
From a boy that isn't your friend?
It's driving you, me and Mum round the bend.

This is what the letter says!
'To . . .
Roses are red,
Sugar is sweet
Which I like to eat,
Violets are blue,
Which I never knew!'

This letter is from somebody
But why should I tell you!

Emma Thomas (10)
Carswell Primary School

The Running Mouse

The running mouse,
Ran around,
Running away from the hungry cat,
Over the log,
Over the mat,
The hungry cat got stuck in a mat.

The running mouse,
Ran outside,
Running away from the hungry cat,
Past the forest,
Past some rats,
The hungry cat was stuck by rats.

The running mouse,
Took a break,
A rest from the hungry cat,
On the log,
Looked back,
The hungry cat fell flat.

Thomas Wilkinson (9)
Carswell Primary School

Carswell

C lassroom is filled with people,
A ssessments are always fun,
R eading lots of poems and books,
S chool dinners are delicious,
W ork in school is fantastic,
E verybody in school is nice,
L aughing loud in the playground,
L earning something new every day.

Andrew Vanneck (10)
Carswell Primary School

I Love My Lizard

Little like a pencil,
Over the wall, he's waving his hand,
Very beautiful, more than an angel,
Every time trying to talk to me.

My little friend,
You will always be mine.

Lizard, lizard, where are you?
I love you very much,
Zig zag all the way,
Always sitting quietly,
Running to hide for hide-and-seek,
Down in the . . .

Constant Afun (10)
Carswell Primary School

Town Sounds

I am the traffic in the town
That beeps, beep beep, beeps, beep beep.

And we are the shoes that
Tap, tap tap, tap, tap tap.

We are the slamming doors in shops,
Slam, slam slam, slam, slam slam.

And we are the shoes that
Tap, tap tap, tap, tap tap.

We are the people in shops and cafes,
Chitter chatter chitter, chitter chatter chitter.

And we are the shoes that
Tap, tap tap, tap, tap tap.

Penny Gray (7)
Carswell Primary School

Seaside Sounds

We are the children at the seaside,
Splashing in the sea, splashing in the sea.

And we are the waves,
Crashing and bashing, crashing and bashing.

We are the boats on the sea that
Boom, pop, boom, pop, pop.

And we are the waves,
Crashing and bashing, crashing and bashing.

We are the seagulls at the seaside,
Screech and squawk, screech and squawk.

And we are the waves,
Crashing and bashing, crashing and bashing.

We are the rocks at the seaside,
Clatter clock, clatter clock.

And we are the waves,
Crashing and bashing, crashing and bashing.

Thomas Mullord (7)
Carswell Primary School

Valentine's Day

Love is in the air
Over everywhere
Valentine's Day is here again
Everyone insane.

Live in a nice house
Over the beautiful sky
Valentine's Day is a beautiful day.

Kyle Wilde (9)
Carswell Primary School

Seaside

I am the sand at the seaside,
Tinkle, crinkle, tinkle, crinkle.

And I am the sea that
Wishes and washes, wishes and washes.

We are the ice lollies
Slurp, slurp slurp, slurp, slurp slurp.

And I am the sea that
Wishes and washes, wishes and washes.

We are the dogs at the seaside,
Woof and bark, woof and bark.

And I am the sea that
Wishes and washes, wishes and washes.

I am the seaweed at the seaside,
Pop and crackle, pop and crackle.

And I am the sea that
Wishes and washes, wishes and washes.

Joseph Morgan (8)
Carswell Primary School

Hot Day At The Beach

Sun is yellow, sun is bright,
You can go to the beach any time you like,
Crystal clear blue sea,
I think I might just take a swim,
Invite your friends for a swim
And then let's go and have ice cream.

Adi Lusiana Wainiqolo (10)
Carswell Primary School

Town Sounds

We are the birds in the city,
Chirp a-chirp, whistle, chirp a-chirp, whistle.

And I am the traffic,
Beep a-beep beep, beep a-beep beep.

We are the people in the city,
Chitter, chatter chatter, chitter, chatter chatter.

And I am the traffic,
Beep a-beep beep, beep a-beep beep.

We are the cars in the city,
Broom a-broom broom, broom a-broom broom.

And I am the traffic,
Beep a-beep beep, beep a-beep beep.

Mitchell Curtis (8)
Carswell Primary School

My Dog Hal

My dog Hal,
Is one of my best pals,
I love taking him for a walk,
But sometimes it's just an excuse for a talk.

I love my dog,
He's a bit scared of frogs,
He loves playing with his sister,
When she got taken away from the litter,
I suppose he missed her.

Caroline Church (10)
Carswell Primary School

City Sounds

We are the bags in the city that
Rustle and tussle, rustle and tussle.

And I am the traffic that
Zooms and booms, zooms and booms.

We are the wind in the city that
Blows but goes, blows but goes.

And I am the traffic that
Zooms and booms, zooms and booms.

We are the children in the city
Chatter, chatter chatter, chatter, chatter chatter.

And I am the traffic that
Zooms and booms, zooms and booms.

We are the people in the city that
Stamp and tramp, stamp and tramp.

And I am the traffic that
Zooms and booms, zooms and booms.

Chloe Frame (8)
Carswell Primary School

Town Sounds

We are the people in the town,
Mutter and mumble, mutter and mumble.

And we are the vehicles that
Rach a char, rach a char.

We are the raindrops in the town,
Drip drop, drip drop.

And we are the vehicles that
Rach a char, rach a char.

Emily Cackett (7)
Carswell Primary School

Sounds At The Seaside

We are the waves in the sea
That swish swash swish, swish swash swish.

And we are the boats that
Toot a-toot toot, toot a-toot toot.

We are the children in the sea
That slash, slosh, slash, slosh.

And we are the boats that
Toot a-toot toot, toot a-toot toot.

We are the wind in the sky
That blows and blows, blows and blows.

And we are the boats that
Toot a-toot toot, toot a-toot toot.

We are the people on the beach
That call people's names, call people's names.

And we are the boats,
Toot a-toot toot, toot a-toot toot.

Cassidy Sandall (8)
Carswell Primary School

Sounds Of The City

We are the cars in the city that
Broom, a-broom, broom, broom.

And we are the traffic crossings that
Beep and flash, beep and flash.

And we are the trains in the city that
Choo choo choo, choo choo choo.

And we are the traffic crossings that
Beep and flash, beep and flash.

We are the people in the city that
Walk and talk, walk and talk.

We are the traffic crossings that
Beep and flash, beep and flash.

I am the music in the city that
Rings and tings, rings and tings.

We are the traffic crossings that
Beep and flash, beep and flash.

Jade Bates (7)
Carswell Primary School

Village Sounds

We are the whistling of the birds in the village
That tweet, tweet tweet, tweet, tweet tweet.

And we are the beeping of the cars,
Beep a-beep beep, beep a-beep beep.

We are the drains in the village that
Gurgle gurgle gurgle, gurgle gurgle gurgle.

And we are the beeping of the cars,
Beep a-beep beep, beep a-beep beep.

We are the cows on the farm that
Moo a-moo moo, moo a-moo moo.

And we are the beeping of the cars,
Beep a-beep beep, beep a-beep beep.

Katie Shaw (8)
Carswell Primary School

Park Sounds

We are the swings in the park that
Creak and rattle, creak and rattle.

And we are the children that
Scream and shriek, scream and shriek.

We are the mummies in the park
Chatter, chatter, chatter, chatter.

And we are the children that
Scream and shriek, scream and shriek.

We are the see-saws in the park
Bang and bump, bang and bump.

Rebecca Cooper (7)
Carswell Primary School

School Sounds

We are the doors in the school
Slam and bang, slam and bang.

And we are the feet that
Stomp and stamp, stomp and stamp.

We are the children that
Scream and shout, scream and shout.

And we are feet that
Stomp and stamp, stomp and stamp.

We are the teachers in school that
Shout and shout, shout and shout.

And we are the feet that
Stomp and stamp, stomp and stamp.

We are the workmen that
Clang and bang, clang and bang.

And we are the feet that
Stomp and stamp, stomp and stamp.

Sarah Greenaway (8)
Carswell Primary School

Park Sounds

We are the ladders in the park,
Bang, bang bang.

And we are the swings that
Clatter and clatter, clatter and clatter.

We are the slides in the park,
Scrape, scrape scrape.

And we are the swings that
Clatter and clatter, clatter and clatter.

We are the gates in the park that
Slam, slam slam.

We are the see-saws that
Squeak, squeak squeak.

And we are the swings that
Clatter and clatter, clatter and clatter.

Tamsin Harling (8)
Carswell Primary School

Down The Mountain

I snowboard down the mountain,
It's really fun,
I go really fast,
There's no need to run.

I zoom down the mountain,
On my pair of skis
And the only things whizzing past,
Are the people and trees.

I go up the mountain,
In a cable car,
I see people going down,
We're up the mountain very far.

Cameron Jon Exeter (9)
Chipping Warden Primary School

My Pet Dog

Every day I see my dog Barney running up the garden,
Barking all day long when a car goes past,
Rolling about on his back when he's got an itch,
He is naughty though, when he escapes in the little places.

He likes playing football with his nose,
Sometimes plays with the hose,
We take him out on walks,
He barks and barks and barks.

He will get under your feet,
He is as white as snow,
He is a Westie though,
And as playful as anything.

When he's in with the snow,
We can hardly see him,
He will raid the bins,
And climb up logs,
After all, he is my favourite dog.

Thomas Laxton (10)
Chipping Warden Primary School

Countryside And Village

The birds chirp in the tree,
The cool air brushes past me,
In the tree there is a bee,
Making honey for his tea.

From the morning comes dark,
In the foggy distance I see a park,
I run towards it very fast,
All the houses going past.

Now it's dark,
I must go to bed,
When I get home I'll rest my head,
With my cuddly, warm ted.

I'm finally tucked up in bed,
Finally can rest my head,
Then I yawn very loud and . . .
Zzzzzzzzzzzz!

Anna Nash (10)
Chipping Warden Primary School

Manchester United

Me and Ollie are fans of Man U,
They're first place in the premier league,
My favourite player is Ruud Van Nisterooy,
He's the best scorer for Man U.

Me and Ollie want to be as good
As Ruud Van Nisterooy when we're older,
We go to every home game they go to,
Apart from when they play in Birmingham.

Me and Ollie used to like David Beckham,
But unfortunately he moved to Real Madrid,
Man U are going to beat Arsenal,
And in the end we did.

Benjamin Edwards (10)
Chipping Warden Primary School

Music

Semibreves and crotchets
Are very easy to play,
But quavers and minims you will really
Need all day.

I play the violin
Harriet plays it too,
I really think if you tried it
You could do it too.

Chloe can play the recorder
She shares a stand with me,
The only note she cannot do
Is probably the note C.

Sometimes we play in assembly
It really is quite fun,
But sometimes I'm quite pleased when
It's all over and done.

Abbie McCammond (9)
Chipping Warden Primary School

Down The Field

Down in the fields,
Amongst the bright green grass,
With cows chomping away,
The wind blows through the trees,
You can hear the whistling.

The sun starts to go down,
You head home,
Open up the gate,
Kick off your wellies,
Snuggle down by the fire.

Esme Stanley (9)
Chipping Warden Primary School

Yellow

Yellow is the sun, bright at mid-day,
Yellow is a sunflower, fragrant as can be,
Yellow is the sand, shimmering on the beach,
Yellow is the bin, where you throw away rubbish.

Yellow is the lemon, sour and bitter,
Yellow is a banana, soft and squishy,
Yellow is butter, melted on toast,
Yellow is an egg yolk, scrambled for breakfast.

Yellow is paper, crisp to draw on,
Yellow is a book, full of a good story,
Yellow is a box to carry things in,
Yellow all around us, that's what I like.

Chloe Cox (9)
Chipping Warden Primary School

My Friend . . .

My friend Abbie has a cat called Moby
My friend Harriet has a pet pony
My friend Kirsty has a pet hamster
I have a pet gerbil
But my auntie has none of these
She has a baby boy instead.

My friend Gaby has a big brother
My friend Katy has a little brother
My friend Alex has a big sister
My friend Sophie has a little sister
But I am the odd one out
I haven't even one sister, poor me!

My friend Millie likes pizza
My friend Hannah likes pasta
My friend Helen likes pizza too
My friend Tara likes hot dogs
And so do I!

Sarah Biegel (7)
Chipping Warden Primary School

The Day of the Forest

Awakening mist,
The sun shining through the trees.
The soft tweeting of birds,
Underfoot the leaves, soft and crunchy.

Creatures stir,
Suddenly the forest is alive.
Leaping deer, singing birds,
The forest awakens.

Then, mysteriously,
Everything is silent.
The sun sets,
And the forest sleeps.

It's the same as that,
Every day.
But really, something is moving,
Could it be . . . could it be?

Cassie Forbes (8)
Chipping Warden Primary School

Mountain

I'm climbing up the mountain
Hoping not to fall,
Dropping down, down
That's the worst thought of all.

I'm climbing up the mountain
It's getting misty up here,
I keep on thinking what to do
When the top is near.

I've climbed up the mountain
I've stuck the flag in the turf,
I'm at the top this very moment
Now I've got to go back down to earth.

Libby Grant (9)
Chipping Warden Primary School

Riding School

Instructors calling out people's names,
Ponies whinnying from the stable door,
Riders stroking horses' faces,
The groom silently sweeping the floor.

Horses' hooves walking along the sand,
Ponies munching up their hay,
The sound of someone pouring water,
The muffled voice of 'neigh, neigh!'

Then the owners come to say goodnight,
The click as the instructor turns off the light,
The bang of doors being locked,
The silent mutter of 'goodnight!'

Harriet Clarke (9)
Chipping Warden Primary School

Autumn Time

The weather is getting quite cold,
The leaves are falling on the ground.
Orange, red and brown, no green leaves around,
People planting pumpkin seeds ready for Hallowe'en.

Animals making their cosy beds for their winter sleep,
Birds flying to the hot countries far away from the cold.
Children having hot chocolate at night to keep them nice and warm,
People going to bed early as the nights are getting dark.

Children jumping in the leaves that have fallen on the ground
Little ones are practising for the nativity play.
Receptions are getting used to school now they are there for a
                                                    whole day,
The juniors are practising for their play.

Autumn is here to stay.

Lily Waddington (9)
Chipping Warden Primary School

My Nanny's Dog

My nan's dog is biteful,
My nan's dog is playful,
My nan's dog is always full of energy,
Her name is Ellie.

My nan's dog is white,
Her eyes are full and bright,
But sometimes she has a fright,
Her name is Ellie.

My nan's dog will eat anything,
She'll sleep on anything,
She'll even bite anything!
Her name is Ellie.

Alex Buck (10)
Chipping Warden Primary School

Hobbies

Everyone has different hobbies,
My hobby is art, I find it fun,
People have different hobbies,
But art is mine.

Abbie's hobby is walking dogs,
Thomas' hobby is golf,
Alex's hobby is football,
My teacher's hobby is gardening.

So there are some hobbies,
Very different to mine,
Yet everyone has their own hobby,
What is yours?

Roxanne Clarke (9)
Chipping Warden Primary School

A New Day

Ship sailing in
and dolphins with a fin
waves crashing on the beach
seagulls flying out of reach.

And as dusk breaks
you can only see
a little yellow light flashing.

In the morning you are woken
by a seagull cawing and moaning
cars bustling in the streets.
A new day begins.

Oliver Mason (9)
Chipping Warden Primary School

Crazy Frankie

Crazy Frankie's round the twist.
Cross him off your party list.
He'll kick your cat
And call your nan a 'dirty rat'.

He'll pop your tyres,
Break your bat,
Mix you jigsaws,
Pull you curtains down.

He'll cut your mum's night-gown
And the worst thing he'll do is call you a 'dirty louse'.
Crazy Frankie round the twist,
So cross him off your party list.

Oliver James Macdonald-Brown (10)
Chipping Warden Primary School

The Dog Walk

The wilderness of the wild woods
Legs chomping like a lawnmower through nettles
Wild blackberries shining like jewels in the sunlight
Foxgloves like a purple lake.

Midday now
Relaxing on a huge tree
The dog is jumping in the meadows
Chasing a hare much too fast for his old legs.

Growing darker
Long winding roads lead our path home
Cars shooting past like bullets from a gun
Getting into the house now, is that my tea? Yum-yum.

Jack Travis Waterhouse (10)
Chipping Warden Primary School

What Is Gymnastics?

Backflip, frontflip,
Handstand, cartwheel,
That's what gymnastics is,
Back bends, kick overs,
It's so much fun,
I hate it when it's done.

Beam and bars and trampoline,
They are all good for tricks,
Competitions are really good fun,
Badges and trophies to be won,
Get on your kit it's time to go,
It's fun for everyone.

Jumps and kicks,
Flips and tricks,
Spinning round, round and round,
Until you are quite dizzy,
It really is good fun.

Emma Rogers (10)
Chipping Warden Primary School

Animals From Around The World

Bees making honey, high up in the trees,
Salmon spawning down the streams and rivers,
Lions roaring out on the plains,
Frogs leaping here and there,
Pelicans scooping up lots of fish,
Spiders scuttling all around the place.

Falcons swooping, catching lots of food,
Wallabies escaping forest fires,
Armadillos curling into balls,
Penguins huddling in big groups,
Great whites attacking seals and sea lions,
Dolphins chasing fish all day.

Wolves howling in forests and woods,
Sea lions playing with bouncy balls,
Tigers roaring, chasing prey,
Lizards basking in the sun,
Wildebeests charging at full speed,
Foxes scavenging night and day.

Rhinos escaping poachers by running very fast,
Bats sleeping through the day,
Crocodiles waiting for some prey,
Snakes slithering through the sand,
Pigeons escaping sparrowhawks,
Dragonflies hovering above ponds.

Daniel Spring (9)
Chipping Warden Primary School

The Garbage Gobbler

Munch, munch, gobble, gobble!
The garbage gobbler roams around,
He's covered in spots,
Black and dark and mouldy,
Like potatoes in an old brown sack.

He eats old crisp packets,
All kinds of foul-smelling rubbish,
Tin cans, jam jars, old pieces of rope,
Measuring tape, potato peelings,
Everything we don't want.

Sadly, one day,
He ate so much he exploded,
Never to be seen again,
Yet on dark nights you can hear
His faint munch, munch, gobble, gobble!

Sophie Biegel (9)
Chipping Warden Primary School

Beyond The Door

Go and open the door.
Maybe outside there's a fallen star on the branch of a tree
Or a flying unicorn with shiny wings.
Go and open the door.
Maybe there's the end of the world, scary and dark.
Maybe the end of the rainbow, magical and sparkly
Or a dragon's cave under the ground,
Or a one-eyed Cyclops, with a wooden club.
Go and open the door.
If you dare.
It might be scary.

Patrick Pearce (8)
Crowmarsh Gifford Primary School

The Charge Of Northampton Town
(Based on 'The Charge Of The Light Brigade' by Alfred Lord Tennyson)

Half a mile, half a mile,
Half a mile onward.
Into Old Trafford,
Rode eleven underdogs.

Forward the red brigade.
'Ravish that team!' he said.
'Capture those legs,' he said.
'And Barthez could blunder.'

Giggs to the left of them,
Scholes to the right of them,
Solskjaer in front of them,
Cherries out numbered.

Flash down the left wing,
Giggs' shot has such a sting.
Cutting through the defenders there,
Tricks and flicks, everywhere.
Old Trafford wonders.

Plunged through the cherry bloke,
Right through the line they broke,
Harsley and Weaver reeled from the master's stroke
Shattered and defeated.
They walked head held low,
Morale and strength depleted.

When can their glory fade?
O the attempt they made.
All Old Trafford wondered.
Honour the claim they made,
Honour the game they played,
Noble yet sundered.

Joshua Bennett (9)
Crowmarsh Gifford Primary School

Weather

The sun is Peter Pan's pirate ship flying in the solar system,
The moon is a marshmallow with burnt edges,
The stars are the last of a great fire flickering in the ashes,
The lightning is an alien's torch shining in its attic,
The thunder is an angel's drum playing the night away,
The clouds are candyfloss in a blue wrapper,
The rainbow is hundreds and thousands arranged on a blue plate.

Evie Stretch (8)
Crowmarsh Gifford Primary School

The Devil

Twisting its body round and round,
Its body lurching
As it searches for prey,
The snake, devil's pet.

Its mouth a slimy cauldron,
Bubbling softly in the heat.
Its body lunging this way and that
As it looks for revenge,
The dragon, devil's idol.

Two blood-red horns,
A cruel hand not sparing its whip.
Laughing evil laughs
To his slaves from Earth.
    The Devil.

Alexandra Ball (11)
Crowmarsh Gifford Primary School

Busy Streets

Yellow taxis passing by
Beep beep
Need to get there on time
Police car going by to stop a crime
Buses going by to drop people off
Pick people up, people trying to get to work on time
Lorries going by dropping parcels off
Postmen running door to door
Dropping letters through letter boxes.

Jack Whelan (10)
Crowmarsh Gifford Primary School

Elegant Spring

The bare trees flourish with wonderful blossom,
As her gentle voice stimulates the beautiful morning,
She will not hold back her flowing kindness,
But lets a quilt of flowers restore.

The sun shines like her twinkling eyes,
As her innocent smile returns.
The miniature seeds creep out
And her timid face gleams.

Just as the bulbs are sprouting,
The time comes round again,
But her pleasing voice sings with beauty,
As spring dies down with a delicate touch.

She softly sways back to her burrow
Where she will elegantly sleep,
Until it is the time,
For her beauty to bloom again.

Rebekah Hoodless (10)
Crowmarsh Gifford Primary School

A Very Hot Curry

There was a young man from Surrey,
Who ate a very hot curry.
Later that morning
He found himself yawning
And drinking water in a hurry.

Daniel Sadler (11)
Crowmarsh Gifford Primary School

Limericks

One day in a small town on Skye
A finger turned up in a pie,
Then a nose and two lips,
Then a fine pair of hips,
Then a waitress jumped out and said, 'Hi!'

There once was a man called O'Brien
Who whatever he did kept his tie on:
In the shower, or deck chair,
He was heard to declare
That 'It shows I'm a man to rely on!'

Sammy-Jo Knowles (11)
Crowmarsh Gifford Primary School

Hot And Freezing?

There was a young man from Surrey
Who ran round the house with a hurry
I called his name James
But he burst up into flames
Because of a freezing McFlurry.

James Kennedy (11)
Crowmarsh Gifford Primary School

12 Things Found In A Teacher's Desk

A love letter from her boyfriend to say that he loves her
A tatty pencil case made out of fur

An old homework sheet and
Two rusty screws from the back of a seat

An old football whistle and
The spiky head of a thistle

A fluffy diary from Year 9
And a watch that no longer tells the time

A cosmetics bag to make her look beautiful and
A text book that is no longer suitable

A pair of broken glasses and
Some dried flowers that need vases.

Natasha Jarvis (10)
Crowmarsh Gifford Primary School

The Marble Jar

The tension is mounting,
For the marble counting.

The school's tried so hard,
For a piece of card.

Every single scholar
Is waiting for the honour.

The teacher for Class R,
Opens up the marble jar.
10 for Class R!

So it goes on for all of the classes,
The teachers' teeth gritting behind their glasses . . .

'Ooh, aah, is it us? That's more than we've got.'
Well done Class 3!

Melissa Whitehouse (10)
Crowmarsh Gifford Primary School

The Midnight Bus

It only happens once at night,
When wolves howl and hyenas fight.
It sounds like an engine staggering on,
Down from the stars that really shone.
Down from the moonlight, down from the sky,
Onto the pavement it passes by.
Then it struck me, it's the midnight bus,
All my friends, they made such a fuss
About this tale, but it's really true,
But remember, keep it between me and you.

Thomas Earl (9)
Crowmarsh Gifford Primary School

The London Underground

The London under-*clitter-clatter* ground
Swoosh! Is a right *pain* in the *next stop Waterloo!*
It is so *busy* and is so *loud* as a baboon exercising his *screech!* lungs.
I just *can't* understand why it was *beep-bop!* invented.
Kensington High Street!
I prefer places that aren't so *squelch!* smelly
I really think -
The doors are now closing!
Hey, but that's *my* stop! Wait!
Beep-bop!
No!
    Bother.

Miriam Johnson (10)
Crowmarsh Gifford Primary School

Colonel Fazackerly

Colonel Fazackerly sat down with a drink,
He said to his waiter, 'I need to think,
Bring me that ghost, his name is Sir Marty,
Go and invite him to my big party.'

The waiter said, 'The ghost, he is sorry,
As he had to rush off in a huge hurry.'
Colonel Fazackerly swore, 'That is not right,
He just disappeared out of all sight!'

Chloe Rodwell (11)
Crowmarsh Gifford Primary School

The Weather

Mum, when's the sun going to come out and play?
I've been waiting all day.

Tell me something I don't know
Or is it beginning to snow?

Hey look at all the raindrops
When's it all going to stop?

Look at all the rain outside
Oops I left teddy on the slide.

Look at all the rain dropping
Isn't it plopping?

Emily Diserens (8)
Crowmarsh Gifford Primary School

Spring

She watches with her beady eyes,
At the sheep in the meadows
At the flower blossom so colourful and bright,
She thought about miserable Winter hidden away.

She blew a soft breeze through the land
The trees swayed together in unison
Winter started to cry, rain crashed down,
But Spring just flicked her golden locks and it ceased.

She sees Summer walking towards her,
She sighs, a gentle breeze blows,
Summer's hair flickers, then returns into place,
Spring is not willing to fight.

As Summer comes closer
The day becomes brighter,
They shake hands
As Spring passes over her duties.

Alix Marshall (11)
Crowmarsh Gifford Primary School

Mum And Me

Since Dad left it's just me and Mum,
She works very hard,
And we have lots of fun.
We go swimming and to the bowlplex
You just never know what Mum will do next.
She gets up in the morning
Still playing the fool,
Then feeds me and clothes me
And sends me to school.

Charlie Phillips (8)
Crowmarsh Gifford Primary School

No Please!

Dear Mum,
No thank you for sending me to camp,
I've now rolled over and got an *(ow!)* cramp.
No thank you for sending me outdoors,
The others here are geeks and bores.

Yes please I'd like to go home with you,
That'll suddenly snap me out of the blues.
Yes please I'd like to stop getting orders,
From men by fires, playing recorders.

No thank you for making me stay here,
I know you know really that danger is near.
Yes please, to camp I'd like to say bye,
But if we get home can I just ask . . . *why?*

From Rosie
PS - If you get a new slip,
For the next camp trip,
Can you please get signing?
Thank you kindly.

Rosie Miller (10)
Crowmarsh Gifford Primary School

Gentle Spring

As she looks back on winter
She touches the grass
With her gentle leafy hand
With a glowing sun shining behind her
Her breath is like a calm breeze.

Amy Cherrill (10)
Crowmarsh Gifford Primary School

Potty Pirates

Potty pirates tall and thin,
Short and fat with a long moustache.
A cat called Jilly and a dog named Jo,
Off we go with a yo ho ho.

Captain Potty shouts his orders
'Come on men you lazy boarders,
Slice the main brace,
Mop the decks,
Come on boys or I'll have your necks.'

So potty pirates set sail for land,
China, America and Japan.
In search of jewels of silver and gold,
To bring back to England to be sold.

Melissa Kalkan (9)
Crowmarsh Gifford Primary School

Snowdrop

In January a snowdrop appears,
Its head's like a drop of fresh fallen snow,
Its leathery wings in the wind blow, blow, blow.

A lovely lazy lantern lays in the snow.

It's a soft silky feather,
It's a snowflake in wintry weather,
Hiding in a wooded glade.

The lovely lazy lantern lays there all alone.

Its petals shaped like a pixie hat,
As it lays on its white soft mat,
While swaying in the breeze.

The lovely lazy lantern lays all alone.

It floats like a cloud
As it stands proud.

Frances Whitehouse (10)
Crowmarsh Gifford Primary School

What Kind Of Key Can It Be?

What kind of key
Swings through trees?
What kind of key
Sneaks bananas from your grasp?
What kind of key
Looks cute and cuddly?
What kind of key
Can it be?

What kind of key
Has a tail for balance?
What kind of key
Opens locks of mischief?
What kind of key
Has jungle relatives?
What kind of key
Can it be?

Answer: monkey.

Eleanor Chappell (11)
Crowmarsh Gifford Primary School

Unknown Music

The soft notes rode with the angels on the high wind,
Smooth, peaceful, even, to my ear.
The notes were like the nightingale's
Sweet summer song full of gladness.

As I sat in peace on the emerald green grass,
The pure music filled me with sweet joy and happiness.
The simply heavenly music entered my soul,
Giving me the food of life to have great trust in him.

Olivia Sherry (10)
Crowmarsh Gifford Primary School

Rush Hour!

Monday morning at eight am,
A new day's started rush hour again,
People try to get to work and school,
Stuck in traffic drivers beep their horns.

Getting cross as Big Ben strikes nine,
Haven't moved an inch when you're waiting in the line,
Children trying to cross the busy road,
The lollipop lady looks really cold!

Finally the traffic, it starts to move,
The noise quietens as you settle in your classrooms,
But as it gets to four pm,
The rush hour . . . it starts again!

Ella Bodeker (10)
Crowmarsh Gifford Primary School

Ten Things Found In A Fairy's Pocket

Pink blossom to put in her hair.
A wonderful wand with a star at the top.
An invitation to a ball in a tiny envelope.
A toadstool to sit in a fairy ring.
A dandelion clock to tell the time.
A daisy chain bracelet to wear on her wrist.
A little book of fairy spells.
Magic dust that grants wishes.
A spare pair of wings for emergencies
And an old pair of tatty ballet shoes.

Tahlia Freya Parrett (7)
Crowmarsh Gifford Primary School

Big Fat Toad

I was walking down the road
When I saw a big fat toad
Not one, a big fat load
I said, 'Mr Toad what is your name
And do you live in the rain?
And my name is Mat Plain
I'm going to keep you.'
'No don't, I've got flu.'

Harry Turner (7)
Crowmarsh Gifford Primary School

The Big Performance

I was feeling fine,
Most of the time,
As the concert got nearer,
I could see it clearer,
This challenge ahead of me,
But I know I have the key,
Practise is the thing,
What happens if I break a string?
When I got ready,
I was feeling steady,
I packed up my guitar,
Then we went off in the car,
The lighting was dim,
And there were lots of people coming in,
People were playing their instruments
And singing with contentment,
It was nearly my turn to play
And I've been thinking about it all day,
I was on the stage
And I turned to my page,
I took a deep breath and started to play,
I felt I was about to cast away.

Bradley Hedges (9)
Kirtlington CE Primary School

Cinderella

There was once a little lady, with three sisters
With all the cleaning, she has blisters
Horrible sisters they really are
But she is the best by far

All the sisters go out for a rest
She has to clean but she's the best
When they go out the room's in a mess
When they come back the room looks the best
She has to start the messy floor
After that she starts on the horrible door

All the sisters go out to a posh dance
Cinderella wants to go but there isn't a chance
The fairy comes down and sees what's the matter
I can't go to the dance 'cause my sisters think I'm fatter

Oh gosh! Your clothes are a mess
Let's go get you a beautiful dress
Go on get in the pumpkin carriage
Don't worry it's not as smelly as a garage

Her sisters saw her at the posh dance
Cinderella was dancing with a boy called Lance
She runs out of the dance all so sad
The sisters are really mad
On the way out she loses her shoe
In the horrible piece of goo

A lovely boy comes to the clean door
And sits down on the floor
She puts on the shoe with the gold on the side
And goes for a kiss outside.

Harriet Owen (10)
Kirtlington CE Primary School

Sailing To Death

The great ship of the seas is sailing,
The round red sun is failing,
The cold ocean wind gives a bite,
A great huge storm is in sight.

Men are dying and their wives begin to mourn,
A bolt of lightning shoots down as the sails are torn,
The tall brown mast creaks and eventually snaps,
The sails are set loose and off they flap.

They lose control as the ship hits rocks,
Seagulls are quickly fleeing in their flocks,
'Girl overboard!' cried a woman, 'it's my daughter,'
Slowly the ship slipped out of sight beneath the water.

Away the survivors swim, on the horizon there's land,
People are getting sucked under in the current that none could stand,
They reach the land barely alive,
With no food they didn't have a chance to survive.

Douglas Haynes (9)
Kirtlington CE Primary School

The Phantom Of The Graveyard

The gruesome phantom wakes from the dead
Out of the ground he has no head
He barges through the churchyard door
Up the stairs and through the walls
As the phantom reaches the top
He screams for help he cannot stop
As he screams he wakes the dead
They come out the ground with no hands or legs
They all hover along the ground to wake more dead.

Elliott Sargent (9)
Kirtlington CE Primary School

The Barn Owl

The barn owl awaits on its stump
Waiting for its prey to come and thump
When along comes a scuttle, a rattle of a mouse
Away he scoops through the leaves
But still the mouse carries on in its dreams
And the barn owl swoops down
But still carrying on goes the mouse
Through the apple tree leaves
He pants, but still going on
Up the ragged rocks and down the steep slopes
Away he goes trying to escape

But down comes the owl, the mouse just in front
Trying to get away down the tunnel
Here enters the owl at the start of the funnel
Poor old mouse got eaten beside his own tunnel.

Harriet Hunter (9)
Kirtlington CE Primary School

The Last Knight

Down in the courtyard there stands a gallant knight,
Mounted on his charger getting ready to fight.
He stretches out; and grabs his lance,
Then gets back to his fighting stance,
He raises his helmet onto his head,
Now his steed starts to tread.

The young bold knight raises his hand,
Then was lit the fiery brand.
The gate was lowered to the floor,
From the castle came a roar.

Out he rode to the battlefield,
He raised his lance, he raised his shield.
His armour glimmered under the sun,
This battle he knew could not be won.

Patrick Hunter (11)
Kirtlington CE Primary School

Jack And The Beanstalk

Jack goes to market.

Jack went to market one day.
He met a man on the way.
He said, 'I will buy your cow
But I've got no money right now.'

Jack sells the cow.

He added, 'I've got some beans on me
That will grow into a massive big tree.'
Jack said, 'The beans sound great.
I will sell the cow for eight.'

Jack plants the beans.

Jack showed the beans to his mum.
She thought they were real dumb.
Jack said, 'Mum I beg your pardon
But I'm going to plant them in our garden.'

Jack climbs the beanstalk.

Jack looked out of the window up high
To find the plant had grown up to the sky.
His mum told him to take a long walk,
But instead he decided to climb the beanstalk.

Gareth Preston (10)
Kirtlington CE Primary School

Jack And The Beanstalk!

Jack goes out to sell the cow on a cold and frosty morning
He meets a man, who asks the way just as the day was dawning

That's a fine cow you have young sir
Will you accept these beans for her?

I don't know if my mum will agree
But these are magic beans the man said with certainty

Jack takes the beans home to his mum
You stupid boy how can you be so dumb?

She took the beans and flung them out
And landed Jack with a thumping clout

Jack was sent to bed without any bread
Nursing his feelings and a very sore head

Next morning, where the beans were thrown
A humongous, beautiful beanstalk had grown.

Zac McEachran & Charlie Brinkworth (9)
Kirtlington CE Primary School

The Haunted Castle

The boy was asleep lying on his bed,
And all he could feel was a tap on his head,
He ran really fast out of his room,
But he knew he was going to get caught soon,
He tried to run to his mum's bedroom,
But she was out under the moon,
He tried to get out of the back door,
But then he tripped and he was really sore,
He ran upstairs to try and hide
And when he got to the place he cried,
The ghost looked in and saw his head,
'Now I've found you you're going to be dead.'

Josh McEachran (10)
Kirtlington CE Primary School

Freddy Bing

There once was a man who shot wooden arrows
And still had the time to roll around on barrows
He is one of a kind
He always helps the blind
He rides in green what's his name
The villains he meets oh they're lame
He is actually quite a mysterious guy
He knows everyone so he always says hi
He is called Freddy Bing
He also collects nice rings
Once he defeated Madam Helen
His favourite fruit is watermelon
Then one day pirates came
They are not good they are quite lame
Then they challenged us to a fight
However, we did not know that they bite
When I woke up the next day
The pirates had left and left the bay
They took that as a warning
And celebrated the next morning
So hip hip hooray for us
We went somewhere on a bus
We drank loads of beers
And aren't going back for years.

Nicole Beahan (10)
Kirtlington CE Primary School

Shipwrecked

The big black ship comes sailing, sailing,
All the men on board are nailing, nailing.
'Ouch,' said one sailor, sailor, sailor, 'Ouch,'
And went to sit on the big black couch.
Instead fell out of the big black ship, big black ship,
The other men were amazed as they bit their lip.
'Come and see me soon, soon, soon.'
'Where are you going, the moon, the moon?'
'No I'll swim away to shore, to shore,
To the icy shores of Mr More, Mr More.'

We'll sail away for another day, another day,
And we will reach the end of May.
I'll climb the rigging to see the end of the sea,
Then I'll go and see my mate, *me* yes *me*.
Then the big black ship gave a very loud creak,
While it sailed round a pile of seaweedy rocks.
Then two sailors were flung off the ship,
We will get more than a great big nip.
They fell in the water saying their very last prayers,
No one else seems to care, no one else seems to care.

The sailors left, climbed the rigging to see if they could see,
The land of Africa, as well as sailing over the icy seas.
They spotted Africa in the east, they spotted Africa in the east,
At least they spotted it, at least they spotted it, at least.
They got what they wanted, the main thing was water,
They were crying for water, crying with laughter.
They hit a small island later that very same day,
They decided to stay on that island, yes stay.
They made a small bud last a day or two
And then they heard a great big coo.

Megan Bates (9)
Kirtlington CE Primary School

The Battle Of Helm's Deep

Waiting for battle of elves and men,
Against Uruk-Hai fighting for Saruman in his den.

Over the hillside dead at night,
Uruk-Hai come marching for an evil fight.

Uruk-Hai stop quiet and wait,
But one of the men lets go his arrow and hits his bait.

Men and elves start the battle,
Uruk-Hai come running with spears and make a rattle.

Arrows are shot everywhere killing Uruk-Hai,
While most men to the world say goodbye.

The Uruk-Hai have ladders and climb up,
But Aragorn and his men have swords for luck.

The Uruk-Hai blow up part of Helms Deep,
They track through water with their mucky feet.

King Théoden calls back to the keep,
Uruk-Hai come up steps which are steep.

Aragorn, King Théoden decide to run out,
To the battle they're almighty with no doubt.

They look towards Uruk-Hai,
With swords and axes most of them die.

Just when men and elves are losing battle,
Someone unexpected comes on the saddle.

In the east Gandalf comes with luck,
With riders of Rohan that come down in muck.

They ride down the mountain steep,
On their horses running down 200 feet.

Riders of Rohan, Gandalf, elves and men,
Win the battle against Saruman, who's in his evil den.

Rhys Harris (9)
Kirtlington CE Primary School

I Wish

Down in the garden, where nobody goes
There's a dark secret that nobody knows,
With its biscuit-like paving slabs
Dozens of plant pots over some rags

But down in the garden, on one little daisy
A graceful fairy lived, her name was Maisy,
With her glittery wings, her dainty toes
She rests her head on a beautiful rose

But one day a little girl,
Her teeth gleamed like a pearl,
Her hair lovely, fair and blonde
Her father was very fond

She trotted down to the flower
To the fairy, with all the power,
There she was granted three wishes!
She wished she could swim with all the fishes

Then she flicked back her hair so blonde
Then she landed in the pond,
He wish had finally come true
Now she was swimming in the ocean blue

'Two more wishes or will you spare?'
Then Maisy danced round in the air,
My next wish is to be a cat
But, not one that is very fat!
So I can prowl around night and day
Then at midnight, sleep upon the hay

Now this is my last wish I must get it right
Because the fairy will be gone before midnight
I wish I could have a pony of my own,
To love and to care for and ride all the way home.

Helen Kirby (10)
Kirtlington CE Primary School

The Three Little Pigs

The little pigs left home one day
To make their fortune far away
Mother said, 'Watch out, watch out!
In case the big bag wolf's about!'

The first pig built a house of straw
He went inside and shut the door
The wolf came and blew and blew
The little pig didn't know what to do.

With one big puff the wolf blew the house away
The poor little pig has nowhere to stay.

The second pig built a house of sticks
He wished he had built a house of bricks.
The wolf huffed and puffed and the sticks
Fell, poor little piggy did not feel well.

The third pig built a house of bricks
To stop the wolf and his dirty tricks.
The three little pigs were safe and sound,
No way could this house fall to the ground.

He tried the door but it was locked
He jumped on the roof and the chimney pot
Rocked, he fell through the hole into a hot pot
And that was the end of his nasty plot!

Joe East (8)
Kirtlington CE Primary School

Dragon Tales

There have been tales
Of dragons with scales, on a great stormy night.
But always there,
With long golden hair, a maiden above all the knights.
'Come forth mighty dragon,'
She said, it came staggering, 'Come forth with
All your grind.' Up to the battlefield the dragon rose,
Really, really it was a great pose.

Knights came storming, came storming, came storming,
The battle went on past morning, past morning,
All was lost for the knights of dawning,
They all knew they would die by morning.
That fateful day in the morning,
The knights were yawning in the morning,
Before their doom,
In the afternoon,
A knight came riding his armour all gleaming,
He came to stop his friends from bleeding,
The battle rose on until the evening.

The knight stormed up to the dragon's toes,
He climbed up to the dragon's rows,
Of great metal white teeth
And gave the dragon great, great grief,
He killed the dragon and became chief.

Alex Rogers (8)
Kirtlington CE Primary School

My Poem for You

I am writing this poem to let you know
I think it's quite good!
Do you think so?
I love writing poems as you can see
I've written a whole book of them!
Yep, that's me

I write poems about animals, family and friends
I could go on forever, the list never ends!
Sad poems, happy poems, poems that make me cry
It would take me ages, and that's no lie
Good ones, bad ones, weird ones too!
So that's why I'm writing this poem for you

I'm sitting at the table scratching my head
My mind has gone completely dead!
Dad's standing by the Aga waiting for me to stop
Why is my hand going so hot?
My puppy is waiting for me on the floor
Why is she looking up at the door?
She's waiting for me to finish up
I can't go that fast, so hold on pup!

I've got to go now, time really does fly
It was nice to talk, have the chance to say, 'Hi!'
I hope that you liked the poem you've just read
I really must go now, it's time for my bed!

Daniella Ashdown (10)
Kirtlington CE Primary School

Harry Potter

Harry Potter was running through the old corridor,
He opened the creaky door,
When he flung off his invisibility cloak he looked up and
Saw a headless ghost float,
He was frightened, he said,
'Can I find your head?'
The ghost said, 'Yes please.'
Harry dropped to his knees,
Behind him a cupboard door
Which was tightly closed before,
Opened and a head rolled out.
'Thank you!' the ghost did shout.

Martha Buck Bohan (10)
Kirtlington CE Primary School

A Piece Of Ammonite (Fools' Gold)

I see the top of houses
And the golden mountains
The tips of cliffs
And the shining sun

I see trees of bronze
Buildings so high they touch the clouds
A village lit up with torches
And birds with their shining beaks

I see a turquoise sea
Treasure and fish
Lions and tigers
Bears and lizards
Castles and towers
As long as I am asleep . . .

Felix Frank (8)
Lynams Dragon Pre-Preparatory School

Snow

Snow, snow fantastic snow!
Never before has it been so cold!
Over our heads it comes down fast!
When it comes, I'm never last.

I rush out for a fun cold day to play!
Now it's coming
I must now rush
'Go away snow!' I would never dare to say!

Now
I really
Must
Dash
To get out fast . . .
Out of the house
I'm first in the snow

Wow! It's fun to be out in the snow again . . .

Molly Tang (8)
Lynams Dragon Pre-Preparatory School

The Snake

I see scales on a snakeskin soft and smooth
Coiling in a ring
A sting will not harm him
A snake will eat an earthquake
Yes he will!
A sting will not hurt him
Oh no it won't
He knows how to cling
It's in his head
Don't sneak past him!

Ibrahim Ait Tahar (7)
Lynams Dragon Pre-Preparatory School

Inside My Crystal

I see the moon shining with the stars
It looks like an icicle but twinkling like the moon
I see it flashing blue and green
Then . . .
Wait a second . . .
It's going red!
I see the moon beneath the stars
It's shining bright and very fast.

Oli Rowlands (7)
Lynams Dragon Pre-Preparatory School

Bubbling Hellbroth
(Inspired by Macbeth)

Grind a female's pulse
Pinch the spit of dog
Fry some fresh frogs' legs
And in the charmed pot pour
Boiled tongues
Whiskey dreams
And the face of Anne Boleyn

Peel the school of eyeballs
Grate the rotten slugs
Mix the very green teeth
Under the dark moonlight
Boil and bubble.

Alice Dendy (7)
Lynams Dragon Pre-Preparatory School

Brew To A Bad Life
(Inspired by Macbeth)

Pour the vomit, bubble and stew
Paste the mud thick as glue
Clot the blood, ooh, ooh, ooh,
Peel the eyeballs, thick as walls
Cube the mouse tails
Squeeze the ketchup!
Curl the stings
Change the bad thoughts and the dreams
Into ghostly wails and screams

Fry the sting ray particle and
let
them
sink
Mix the powdered bone with liquid zinc
Use the slime and sludge as an ultra bad side
Pop in Anne Boleyn's pizza (Henry will have his pride)
Sieve on the powdered shark's tooth and let it froth and bubble
Pour in the liquid lead
And top it with the fire
This is the worst brew you will ever have
In your life
It will give you
So much strife!

Miriam Lawson (7)
Lynams Dragon Pre-Preparatory School

Witch's Soup
(Inspired by Macbeth)

We come out and dance under the open moon
We cackle while we cook the helpless school of eyeballs
In that we grind the head of newt
We boil the spit of dog
Then we snap the point of the bloody dagger
Slice the rotten slugs
Grate the puppies' tails
And we *stir* them altogether

We chop the army of ants
And crush the rotten green teeth
We are the witches of wicked dreams
With a warthog's nose
And a dead man's heart!

Flora Cameron Watt (7)
Lynams Dragon Pre-Preparatory School

Eagle

Deep inside the eagle's wing
I see life
I see flight
I see golden feathers
I see the wings of the legendary king of the eagles
I see strength
I see power
I see speed
I see the wing of the true monarch
I see the courage of a thousand men
In one eagle
I see life and heart in one spirit

I see *power.*

Edward Ashcroft (7)
Lynams Dragon Pre-Preparatory School

I See

I see a rainbow droplet drop
Its golden sunshine light
I see a silver bird's wing
It's silky smooth like cloth
I see a scaly python skin
It's as sharp as a dagger!
I see a bluey diamond rock
It's as shiny as a pearl
I see a tiny button
It's whirly in the middle
I see a purple glimmering stone
It glistens in the light
I see a dead tortoise shell
It's stripy, brown and smooth
And you know if you look at them
Carefully
You can really see the moon.

Caitlin Lloyd (8)
Lynams Dragon Pre-Preparatory School

Autumn

Autumn is a beautiful sight
But not in the night.
Leaves are tossed about
Trees are shaking wildly about
Like fierce monsters
But in the day it is much more beautiful
Because it isn't like I just told you
Leaves crackle and sticks go click
And sometimes it is soundless
And the wind whistles
It is praying for brown leaves
And they make the smell of autumn.

Oliver Faulk (7)
Lynams Dragon Pre-Preparatory School

Crash Waves

Waves crash
Waves pierce your ears
Waves crash against giant rocks and make a big
Splash!
Crash waves!
Splash waves!
Bash waves!
Mash waves!
Waves rock boats
Waves break boats
Waves attack boats.

Freddy Creed (8)
Lynams Dragon Pre-Preparatory School

If You Were Alive

I see
Wavy lines
Spikes
Shapes like a diamond
Black and white dots
Why are you wavy around the edges?
How tough were you?
Snakeskin . . .
If you were alive I would ask you . . .
When did you shed your skin?
Which country did you come from?
I wonder what you really look like
What would you eat?
How wide could your mouth open?
Most of you is white.

William Bowen (7)
Lynams Dragon Pre-Preparatory School

Angry Waves

Waves crash and smash and lash
On the seashore
Against the rocks the waves crash and lash and bash
Very angry waves can get you
And they push you over
Every wave is different
They are all shapes and sizes.

Daniel Scott-Kerr (8)
Lynams Dragon Pre-Preparatory School

The Silly Old Woman From Spain

There once was a silly woman from Spain,
Who decided to go on a train,
She hung out the window
And was eaten by a dingo
That silly old woman from Spain.

Kristina Foster (10)
Marcham CE Primary School

My Little Cousins

My little cousins Hugo, Harvey and Jo
I really love them so,
They are lovely little boys
But they make lots of noise,
They're as cute as can be
And they all want to sit on my knee,
That's my cute cousins Hugo, Harvey and Jo.

Georgia Tolley (10)
Marcham CE Primary School

The Sunset

In the sunset secrets lie
Silent stories that'll never die
Peace and freedom
Rule this kingdom
Joy and laughter
Happiness ever after
But as day turns to dusk
And dusk to night
Those hopes and dreams fade . . .
And we're left with reality!

Kathleen Macnee (11)
Marcham CE Primary School

There Once Was A Lady From Mars

There once was a lady from Mars,
Who was obsessed with cars,
She couldn't drive,
Went into a hive,
That silly lady from Mars.

She finally went on a test,
But she didn't do her best,
She didn't get through,
She went boo hoo,
And people say she's a pest.

A few long years went by
And thought she'd have another try
She actually got through,
She went *waa hoo,*
And went back to Mars *bye-bye!*

Georgia Upjohn (11)
Marcham CE Primary School

Farm Animals' Wedding!

I once went to a wedding, it really was a bash
We were sitting in our pew, when we heard a sudden crash
Cows and pigs and donkeys too
All the animals join the crew.
In front of the vicar they said, 'I do'
The pig said nothing but the cow said, 'Moo!'

Soon it came to the yummy feast
The bride yelled louder than a roaring beast
The cake fell down, everyone screamed
But the farmer did not he just beamed
The farmer hates the bride I think you can tell
With all the animals cor what a smell!
When the animals left, the bride was alone
With noting but a fallen cake and an old chicken bone!

Rebecca Rowe (9)
Marcham CE Primary School

Having A Sleepover

Having a sleepover with your friends
All the party fun never ends
You bounce on the bed
Till you feel dead
Then popcorn fights
All through the night
Then finally you can fall asleep
Each eye's open in case the other's aren't asleep
Then suddenly the cockerel rings
Every eye opens with a ping
Everybody groans and moans
It's morning again.

Rosie Ball (9)
Marsh Baldon CE Primary School

Dogs

Playful dogs bark and chase cats,
Scaredy-cats, are dogs scared of bats,
Muddy dogs trail mud on the floor,
Naughty dogs, scratch down the door,
Girly-girly dogs always look clean,
Teasing dogs always play mean,
Lazy dogs laze around in the sun . . .
If I say anymore I'll be killed by a gun!

Holly Barne (9)
Marsh Baldon CE Primary School

The Enchanted Horse

Every night when I go to bed,
I wait and wait until the sky is red,
Then I know the enchanted horse has come.

I run to the cliff that looks over the bay
And the beach that I go to every day,
To meet the enchanted horse and stroke his mane.

I climb onto his back while he stands on the sand,
Then we gallop away to a fantasy land,
The magic enchanted horse, and I.

We eat ice cream and lollies and red strawberry candy,
We both see some foals, whose legs are all bandy,
The enchanted horse and I, have fun.

When the sky is blue we go back home,
I look out of the window and see frothing foam,
The friendly enchanted horse, has gone.

Isabel Barne (10)
Marsh Baldon CE Primary School

The Fire

The fire is a monster of heat,
Who comes from under the grey ash,
It gets higher and higher,
With a blue tint around its body,
To bring heat to all things cold
And then slowly dies down
And goes back into his den.

Robyn Brady (11)
Marsh Baldon CE Primary School

The Moon, The Night And The Stars

The moon is a sparkling snow wolf,
Jumping over the horizon into
The pitch of black satin,
Watching over the world,
His brightness makes the snow
Glitter like diamonds.
The darkness is a black panther
Pouncing into the brightness
Making the world a world of darkness.
The stars are eagle eyes
Watching over the world.

Laurie Davies (10)
Marsh Baldon CE Primary School

Heard It In The Playground
(Written in the style of Ahlberg's Poem)

I heard it in the playground,
I'm going to get you for that,
I'm going to get you for that,
I'm going to tell the teacher,
So give me that back,
Heard it in the playground.

Heard it in the playground,
I really like you,
I really like you,
Heard it in the playground,
Can I play with you?

Sean Brook (10)
Marsh Baldon CE Primary School

A Breakneck Pace

A breakneck pace through technology and science,
A breakneck pace through strikes and defiance,
A breakneck pace laughing and learning,
A breakneck pace into hunger and yearning,
A breakneck pace, rushing through the day,
A breakneck pace in a good and bad way.

A breakneck pace as people get more,
A breakneck pace in a nuclear war,
A breakneck pace saving a life,
A breakneck pace and killed with a knife,
A breakneck pace rushing through each week,
Trying to find the peace we seek.

Harry Greenaway (10)
Marsh Baldon CE Primary School

Heard It In The Playground
(Written in the style of Ahlberg's Poem)

Heard it in the playground,
This is unfair teams,
I heard it in the playground,
Tag you're it,
I heard it in the playground,
I'm going to tell the teacher,
I heard it in the playground,
Make the best team win.

I heard it in the playground,
You're rubbish at football,
I heard it in the playground,
You're not right you're wrong,
I heard it in the playground
Why did you hit it over again?
I heard it in the playground,
Be quiet I'm better than you.

I heard it in the playground,
It's our turn on the climbing frame,
I heard it in the playground,
I can't play my knee's hurting,
I heart it in the playground,
I can't play either,
I heard it in the playground,
Now it's rubbish,
There's only two of us.

Alex Gabbidon (9)
Marsh Baldon CE Primary School

Dazzling Dresses

Spotted dresses play in the sun,
Black dresses have party fun,
Striped dresses like to look tall,
Wedding dresses feel like the belle of the ball,
Ragged dresses climb up trees,
Flowery dresses like afternoon teas,
Short dresses love to show off,
Smelly dresses always blow off,
Winter dresses all nice and cosy . . .
Bang! The shop door closes!

Holly Williams (10)
Marsh Baldon CE Primary School

Kittens

Girly kittens put on blush and lippy
Greedy kittens eat cakes and get sticky
Gorgeous kittens bathe in the sun
Playful kittens laugh and have fun
Lazy kittens snore and sleep
Silent kittens keep secrets deep
White kittens get ready for the ball
Active kittens climb then fall
Motherly kittens fuss over mess
Kind kittens are always the best
Six weeks gone
Ten kittens gone
Miaow!

Emma Stribling (10)
Marsh Baldon CE Primary School

Hammerhead Sharks

H e swims swiftly through the sea
A fter his prey
M illions of fish swim away
M uscles moving in every fish
E ager to kill
R ippling the water as he passes
H e looks above to see seals
E very fish watching his move
A nd every person on the shore
D efinitely watching to see if he's there.

S uddenly he turns
H e spots a seal
A nd eager to get it
R acing to catch it
K ills it
S uddenly it's vanished.

Beth Holdforth (10)
Marsh Baldon CE Primary School

What Is It?

It flies in the skies
It soars with claws
What does it like? A good old fight!

Its friend is a starer but he's not a carer,
It lives in a hole but eats moles,
Annoying all the neighbours with its dashes and capers.

Do you know what it is?

Its vermin squeaks, as it runs the floor creaks,
It lives in a hole
And it's smaller than a mole.

Do you know what it is?

Oliver Fogden (11)
Moulsford Prep School

Pollution

Nuclear power plants are puffing,
People are littering,
Animals are dying,
People are buying,
Animals are crying,
Children are sighing for their pets,
No more pets, no more vets!

Freddie Wilcox (10)
Moulsford Prep School

Wild Animals

On the tips of tall trees, animals are busy gathering food for winter.
In a hurry bugs run from all those big feet
Stamping and squishing all their friends
And thinking about their funerals,
All the birds are singing high in the sky just out of sight,
Making my heart fill with joy.
Out in the wild grass, rabbits hop and jump enjoying themselves
Running, prancing and out-running everything that dares to chase it.
Deep in the water fish swim, twist and turn to avoid the sharks
                                            eating them.

James Boddie (9)
Moulsford Prep School

Winter Snow

The snow was crunching under my feet,
It was quite the opposite to heat.

Snow is cold but fun
It melts when out comes the sun.

Sparkling white
Fun and bright
Snow falls from a great height.

Alasdair Gardiner (10)
Moulsford Prep School

The Park

I was walking on the grass
Looking at the trees and leaves
And staring at a piece of glass
And some bees start to gather.

As I walk across the park
Children start to play and
Insects and animals come for food
And people come today and
As everything grows everything is okay.

The breeze was calm as a bird
And the leaves were as green as ever
And there was a noise which could not be heard.

Alex Bagnall (9)
Moulsford Prep School

Cheetah Cheetah

Cheetah cheetah pumping his heart
Cheetah cheetah like a dart

Cheetah cheetah using his legs
Cheetah cheetah resting his head

Cheetah cheetah camouflaged so well
Cheetah cheetah you will never fail

Cheetah cheetah running for life
Cheetah cheetah dying for a wife

Cheetah cheetah you are so cool
Cheetah cheetah you do not drool

Cheetah cheetah I will love you forever
And hate you *never!*

Charlie Beardall (10)
Moulsford Prep School

Haiku - My Dog

Loving, kind, lazy
Trustworthy, harmless and round
Born a brown Beagle

She licks and cuddles
Whilst sunbathing in the sun
On the rich, green grass

When she is asleep
She dreams she's chasing rabbits
Right down their burrows

When she is happy
Her long brown tail wags a lot
As fast as a pup's

Now the story ends
I hope you have enjoyed it
As much as Prudence.

Charlie Leslau (10)
Moulsford Prep School

An Eagle

Flying through the air,
Moving so swiftly,
Gliding across the sky,
Like he is the king of the world.
Looking down on the clouds and mountains
Where he lives.
Soaring across the sky
So gracefully,
Swooping through the sky,
Feeling unbeatable.
Then departing from the sky
And gracefully landing in his nest.

Richard Leahy (10)
Moulsford Prep School

Snow

Snow snow white and light,
It's crystal clear
And very bright,
Very fun and very bright,
So never get it down your back.

Snow snow white and light,
It's crystal clear
And very bright.
I'll miss it now but I know,
Back at home I can still fly my Moulsford kite.

Snow snow white and light,
It's crystal clear
And very bright.
Now I'm back in the snow,
With the wind having a little blow.

Snow snow white and light,
It's crystal clear
And very bright.
Now I'm skiing
But soon it will be as bright as *night*.

Ben Boddington (9)
Moulsford Prep School

Chocolate

Lovely, creamy, smooth,
In a foil crunchy wrapper,
All sugary and sweet
O hail this great stuff,
The stuff that made Thorntons' shop,
It's the way of life.

Charles Buchan (10)
Moulsford Prep School

The Bloody Battle

As the bloody battle's going,
People dying numbers growing.
As they all go over the top,
Machine-gun fire men shall drop.

The Jerries dig in with the rats,
The allies fly at them like bats.
The Jerry leaders feel like crying,
The ally leaders start their spying.

Kaiser Wilhelm sitting back,
Lets his Jerry goons attack.
Allied soldiers going backwards,
Russian soldiers surging forward.

From Joseph weeping in his hands
For his heir called Ferdinand.
In a cell is Mr Princip,
He's having trouble with his hips.

In the end the Allies won,
Kaiser Wilhelm's reign was done.
Twenty million lives it cost
And a little land was lost.

Sam Rogerson (11)
Moulsford Prep School

My Goldfish

I sometimes watch my goldfish,
When I'm very bored,
He is very fun to play with,
Apart from when he snores.

I think he likes to play with me,
But he can't when I'm not there.
He sometimes likes to spin around
And I think he's like a bear.

I think my fish is very cool,
Especially when he plays with his football.
I like to think of him as a friend,
Even though he's just my pet.

I like my goldfish,
Lots and lots
And I miss him
On my holiday.

Sandy Pain (9)
Moulsford Prep School

Drowning

Falling into darkness, enveloping me
Down underwater dark evil spirits
Pulling me down drowning, drowning
Too small to float too weak to swim
Too tired to scream too lifeless to move
This is the end, oh this is the . . .

Louis Williams (9)
Moulsford Prep School

You Never Get A Second Chance

I really needed some help somewhere,
Because everything was down the drain,
Nothing ever got better.
Until one day,
When everything hit the sky!
I forgot my old life,
A life of greatness came with me,
I forgot my old house,
My old friends,
Everything I'd had before.

Then one day,
After many years,
When I came back to see them,
There was nothing!
It was just a concrete factory,
I remember actually it was great.

The fields, the countryside,
Was there with me.
I knew I'd never be happy again.
I killed myself that afternoon
And sent myself to Hell for what I did.

And I'll never get a second chance.

Felix Newman (10)
Moulsford Prep School

The Best Dog

Millie, Millie the best dog
Millie, Millie is a hog
She will never share her food
She is also very crude

Millie, Millie the best dog
Millie, Millie's a soppy dog
Whenever there's a fire lit
She will sit and stare at it

Millie, Millie the best dog
Millie, Millie the coolest dog
Whenever there's a train going by
She will start to turn one eye

Millie, Millie the best dog
Millie, Millie I love her
When she will die of age
I will simply die of rage.

William Dethridge (9)
Moulsford Prep School

The School Kids' Rap

When the teachers are
Out all day,
All the kids go out and play.

First they rap all around the school,
Then they all go to the pool.

The sixth graders go to the music room,
They get out the drums and make a big boom.

All the teachers return and the kids stop in action,
The teachers put all the kids in detention.

All the kids say, it was our idea to play,
But it was your idea to be out all day!

Auberi Chen (11)
Moulsford Prep School

Nature

Hamsters, hamsters,
Nibble nibble nibble.
Babies, babies,
Dribble dribble dribble.

>Rabbits, rabbits
>Scritch scratch scratch.
>Chickens, chickens,
>From the eggs they hatch.

Trees, trees are
Crashing crashing crashing.
Deers, deers are
Dashing dashing dashing.

>Fish, fish are
>Flipping flipping flipping.
>Foxes, foxes are
>Skipping skipping skipping.

Cats, cats go
Purr purr purr.
We have to take care,
Of nature.

Andrew Grant (11)
Moulsford Prep School

World War I

Oh! The pain of those who died in the trenches of the war,
If only I could have some more, oh if only they could have some more.
As the bombs fell from the sky, oh the pain of those who died,
Each in the rather big, muddy wide.
Oh the sorrows of the dead,
In their deathly bed.
Women and children shall cry,
For their fathers shan't march by.
Oh the dead shall spare a tear,
For my eternal peer.
Oh! The pain of those who died in the trenches of the war,
If only I could have some more, oh if only they could have some more.

Angus Stephen (9)
Moulsford Prep School

What A Dog!

Lottie, Lottie what a dog,
She loves chewing on a log.
She is rolling in the mud,
She is my very best bud.
I like to take her on a walk
And I think she can really talk.
When I get home every day from school,
She gives me a lick nice and cool.
She would never say no to food,
Even if she's in a bad mood.
She likes chasing cats but she wouldn't bite,
She definitely would not get in a fight.
I like throwing Lottie a stick
And I think Lottie is fantastic.

Edward Hughes (10)
Moulsford Prep School

The School

The school, the school,
People learning, people teaching.
The school, the school,
People helping, people playing.

In the classroom, in the school,
People learning, people teaching.
Books and books of everything,
People helping, people playing.

Being naughty at the school,
People learning, people teaching,
Getting justice at the school,
People helping, people playing.

A school outing at the school,
People learning, people teaching,
Coming to a different place,
People helping, people playing.

Summer holidays away from school,
No one learning, no one teaching.
School deserted, no one there,
No one helping, no one playing.

Ben Longden (10)
Moulsford Prep School

The Dragon

The dragon sits on his nest of gold,
This is true or so I am told,
Beauty he does not lack,
The lovely scales upon his back
Shimmer in the evening sun,
A dragon's work is never done,
Fighting knights and magic men,
Taking them to his darkened den.

Luke Gartside (10)
Orchard Close, Sibford School

The End Of Autumn

The sunlight sprinkles on the trees like a cover
of dancing stars.
The orange and gold leaves glow as I walk through
the fallen carpet.
Leaves starting to turn a roasted brown, crisp and
crunching blanket.
The beams of flashing sunlight coming through the trees
The noise of birds getting ready to fly to a warmer climate
fills the air.
The leaves are light and brown, light to the touch and easy to crush.
The bare trees look sadly down through their branches
at the fields around them.
The autumn ground looks like it has been draped with a
cloth of blood.
Leaves sprinkling down like a shower of rain from Heaven
covering the ground around houses.
The sinking sun shines on spiders' webs making shimmering silver
like a calm ocean.
Autumn's end has at last completed the decay of
summer's growth.

David Wells (10)
Orchard Close, Sibford School

Orange

Orange is fire.
Orange is the sun.
A giant ball of flames glowing in the sky.
Orange is warm and comfortable,
And a boiling mass of colour.
Orange is great!

Poppy Tibbetts (10)
Orchard Close, Sibford School

The Magic Of Fog

The fog has come my way,
Just for half a day.
It stayed here until my lunchtime,
Then it went away

I lay down on the floor
Then I began to daydream . . .

I was swimming through the fog,
Searching for the pathway
I was looking all around for the way,
For the pathway down to Earth

And then I found a staircase
I began to descend
If I fell I would fall
All the way back down to Earth

But I liked it in my world
In my foggy, foggy world
Where fog was like the river
I had swum in once before

But then . . .

I was falling
I had slipped
I was no longer in my world,
Swimming through the fog
Searching for the pathway
Looking all around me for the way,
For the pathway down to Earth

I was back on Earth
Where the fog
Had gone away

I was lying
On the floor exactly where
I was before
I went into my world

That is
The magic of *fog*.

Ellie Shercliff (11)
Orchard Close, Sibford School

Winter's Day

Dark grey, foggy clouds
Giant trees like hands
Pathway never-ending disappearing
Into the mist.
Silent, cold, damp world.

Daniel Pickles (11)
Orchard Close, Sibford School

Snow

Fast, glorious, beautiful snow.
Traffic jams, slow cars, people slipping - snow.
Snowmen, children happy, snowball fights - snow.
Everything's white,
    Everything's glittering.
        Everything's lovely.
           That's *snow!*

Samuel Licence (11)
Orchard Close, Sibford School

Seasons

In the winter cold snow falls from nowhere.
Trickling, trickling, trickling
Children excited it's snowing.
Making angels and snowmen
Covering the ground with white powder.
Adults shovelling their way through the drive.
Now the snow is all melting.

It's spring now - all the flowers blooming
Trees growing again
It's warm sometimes
And cold the rest of the time.

It's the hottest time of the year
Rising to almost forty degrees
People going on lovely picnics
The sun hot on their cheeks.

Autumn has come at last
All different colours; yellow, red and orange
Fallen down on the ground like a carpet
At last winter has come for another year.

Ishita Bhatnagar
Orchard Close, Sibford School

My Fog Poem

Hiding things, gone misty grey.
The fog has gone from the trees.
The silence from the birds in the dark bare trees.
Cold misty damp world coming
From the damp snowflakes.

Rory McGill (11)
Orchard Close, Sibford School

Winter

When green turns to white,
It isn't that bright,
It is so gay,
Now let's go and play.

It is so mystical
Don't ring the bell,
Have a snowball fight,
Don't get frostbite!

Joseph Fallon
Orchard Close, Sibford School

The Magic Of A Horse . . .

Their hooves pounding the ground
As they gallop at full speed,
They leap over fences and hedges,
As their beautiful bodies soar through the air.
As they slow to a canter,
You can see their bodies gleam against the sun,
Then slow to a trot and then finally to a walk,
Their heavenly aroma fills the air.
As they lay down to rest,
They turn their backs to the sunset,
The sun goes down as they disappear into the darkness . . .

Deven Pledger (11)
Orchard Close, Sibford School

Sir Hissalot And Sir Kissalaot

Sir Hissalot and Sir Kissalot,
Were invited to a dance,
But Sir Hissalot took his stallion,
And galloped off to France.

Sir Kissalot on the other hand,
Trundled off across the plain,
Upon his patchwork pony,
Grabbing handfuls of its mane.

'Sir Hissalot shall not missalot,'
He said unto his steed,
'But I'm afraid I shall,
And I'm very sad indeed.

Oh bumbling mount, you're far too slow!
You cannot even trot!
Sir Cadogan and his charger
Will be there like a shot!'

When Sir Kissalot arrived,
The dance was in full swing,
The doors burst open,
And he brightly tangoed in.

Sir Speakalot was speechless,
Sir Drinkalot spilt his wine,
The ladies left their partners,
And all gathered in a line.

His shiny shoes were pointed,
His moustache was neatly curled,
He can-canned with the ladies,
And then away he swirled.

Annie Moberly (10)
Rupert House School

When I Had A Dream

One night I had a dream
In the woods I saw a beam
Of light, and in its gentle glow
I saw a horse trot to and fro
And I really could have sworn
That I had seen a unicorn!

A silver lance was on its brow
Made of twisted horn I vow,
Its coat was silver as the moon
And around its hooves were strewn
Golden stars that shone and glowed
I mounted it and off we rode!

We cantered through the old beech trees
Until we came to moonlit seas
Surrounded by some dark, deep caves -
We galloped over shining waves!
I fell off and banged my head
And found that I was still in bed!

Augusta Shaida (9)
Rupert House School

The Miracle Cure

Poor old Granny's sick in bed
'She won't get better,' the doctor said
We gave her a tot of Navy Rum
To settle down her aching tum.

She said she'd have a little more
Because it made her tum less sore,
So we gave her another tot
And pretty soon she'd drunk the lot!

She said 'I'm feeling really great
So let's have more to celebrate.'
We opened up another one,
And all went out to have some fun!

Olivia Knowles (8)
Rupert House School

Christmas

When Christmas is here,
When snow falls from the sky,
When children are sleeping,
When reindeer can fly,
When stockings are hanging,
When Santa is coming,
When stars are twinkling,
When carols are humming,
When presents are waiting,
When frost covers the sheep,
When decorations are pretty,
I'm too excited to sleep!

Laura Bacon (8)
Rupert House School

The Race Between The Sun And The Moon

Bang! Sun's racing,
Moon's pacing,
'Not again!' the stars all sigh.
Sun is winning,
Moon's just spinning,
He has stopped to say, 'Goodbye.'

It's Moon's turn now,
Sun's stopped to row
With a very angry star.
Moon draws ahead,
Sun feels like lead,
What a silly pair they are!

Milly Nunney (8)
Rupert House School

The Family Race

Mum and Dad are having a race
Mum starts off at a very slow pace
Dad's in the lead and going quite fast
Mum still slow and is coming in last
Then my dad gets tripped up by the dog
The sky turns into a terrible fog
It starts to be quite sunny again
And clears away the pouring rain
It looks like Mum is going to win
But then she falls and does a spin
So Dad just leaps right over Mum
I think my dad has clearly won!

Now my sister and I have a race
We both start off in the same place
I get ahead and start to win
I feel so happy I just have to grin
But then I start to slow
My sister barges past and gives me an elbow
But I overtake her - am almost there
My sister does not think that is very fair.

Jessica Miller (8)
Rupert House School

The Pancake Race

Prince John lived in a palace
With his faithful servant James.
They liked to race each other,
And invented silly games!

When it was Shrove Tuesday,
They had a pancake race
The one who won would get a cup,
If they came in first place.

One palace room was really huge,
Eight hundred metres long!
They lined up at the starting line,
They started with a gong!

The floor was very slippy,
James started running fast,
But John ran even quicker,
James was scared that he'd come last.

They started tossing pancakes,
But John flipped his too high!
It landed on the ceiling,
And James went running by!

John's pancake started slipping!
It fell down on the floor!
Poor old John tripped over it,
His bum was rather sore!

He put it in his frying pan,
And ran off at great speed,
But James was running faster,
He still was in the lead!

They soon got near the finish!
The servants cheered them on,
But James stopped to eat his pancake,
So the winner was Prince John!

Victoria Porter (8)
Rupert House School

The Wheelchair Race

The wheelchair race, it was today.
Was I nervous? I should say!
So there were seven others there,
Each was in a fast wheelchair.
Some of us had broken legs
That were fixed with metal pegs.
We didn't mind whether we won
We were there to have some fun!
The sack race finished to a cheer
(All the dads were drinking beer!)
A small girl with pigtails had won,
Her parents clapped and yelled, 'Well done!'
'Wheelchair race people, come up to the line!'
Said a man with a whistle, 'it's nearly time.'
I felt very nervous, got ready to go
I was worried that my wheelchair was slow.
We all went at once, and I raced ahead,
I felt like my wheels had turned into lead!
It was plain to see that I was winning,
While poor old Jane was only beginning,
I was going extremely fast,
While poor Jane, she was coming last!
I rolled the wheels of my wheelchair,
I felt I was flying in the air!
I saw the finish line ahead,
I felt like I was nearly dead!
I raced over the finishing line,
I had won - it felt just fine!

Natalie Jennings (8)
Rupert House School

The Race Day That Went Wrong

Everyone's cheering,
The race has begun!
One hundred metres
They had to run!

Someone's fallen over
But they've got up
They've gone past the finish
Great! They've won the Cup

It's the egg and spoon
And it's gone all quiet
Then all the eggs fall
Oh dear! It's a riot

The sack race is next
It's a very fast pace
The children all trip
And fall flat on their face

The obstacle race
Was a great disaster
The children fell over
And needed a plaster

The eight hundred metres
Went off at a trot
But the leader tripped over
They got tied in a knot

The relay went smoothly
As they ran along
But they mixed up the batons,
And got it all wrong

The visitors' race
Ended up in a scrum
The race day was over
They all had great fun.

Ellen Darke (8)
Rupert House School

The Eating Race

The race was about to begin
I wonder who's going to win
Waiting for the whistle to blow
Look, see the eaters all go
They've all sat down in their places
Ready to stuff their fat faces
For upon their plates they've got
A huge pile of food that is hot
The whistle blew, off they all went
But one person had an accident
For he'd fallen right off his chair
Which gave him a very big scare
As the others were gobbling fast
He knew that he'd come in last
One eater felt terribly sickly
Because he'd eaten so quickly
One person fell off his stool
Because his tummy was rather too full
One started to hiccup so madly
That he started doing quite badly
One who was eating a burger
Cried, 'I can't go any further!'
One person started to choke
For he had drunk too much Coke
While they were chewing and slurping
They all started doing some burping
One by one they gave up
Leaving Sammy to win the gold Cup
But though Sammy was first
He'd eaten so much that he burst!

Yasmin Denehy (8)
Rupert House School

The Race

I was waiting for breakfast,
Lying in bed,
Then I heard a loud sound,
Someone had said:

'Come on people,
She went this way.'
There were sounds of hooves,
And a soft neigh.

I looked out the window,
And here's what I saw,
Five dogs, a fox,
And three horses galore.

Three men sat on the horses,
With rifles in their hand,
Chasing the little red fox,
With their three dogs so grand.

The fox wound round the trees,
Trying to get to her den,
The hunters were chasing her bushy tail,
They wound round again.

The fox was running quite quickly,
The hunters were close behind,
I wanted the fox to win,
As the hunters weren't kind.

The hunters were going to win,
Three gunshots I heard from their gun,
I could not bear to look,
I was sure they had won.

I opened my eyes,
Scared of what I would see,
The fox was cornered,
Against a young tree.

With some stones,
I made a sound,
When the stones hit,
The muddy wood's ground

The hunters looked round,
To see what was the noise,
While I scared the horses,
With my dog's squeaky toys.

The horses sped off,
With the dogs too,
The hunters were yelling
I should, 'Wuh-hoo!'

The fox darted off,
She was able to run,
She got into her den,
The fox had won!

The race was over,
The fox rested her head,
I named the red fox,
And called her Bushy Red.

Amy Nicholas (9)
Rupert House School

The Race

I see a monkey run up a tree.
There's two more and that makes three!
I'll name them, Ned and Fred and Ted.
It's getting late, I'll go to bed.

But I look out and see them race,
Fred is going at quite a pace!
Ned and Ted are catching up,
Who will win the Monkey Cup?

But Fred falls off and bumps his head!
The monkey in the lead is Ned!
Then Ted grabs hold of Ned's long tail,
'This is cheating,' he starts to wail.

But Fred gets up and joins the race
To my surprise, he's second place!
While Ned begins to fall behind,
Ted looks at the sun and then goes blind.

So Fred is now quite well ahead!
Here comes second - it is Ned!
Finally, blind Ted runs past
This poor monkey's come in last!

Laura Bevan (9)
Rupert House School

The Race

On the day of the race,
I woke up in my bed,
I quickly got dressed,
And woke my brother Ted.

It was so exciting,
We both had to rush,
'Get a move on,
Or we'll miss the bus!'

We arrived at the ground,
At the start of the race,
One, two, three *go!*
We set fast pace.

Ted was ahead,
But I soon caught him up,
I was in the lead,
I hoped I'd win the Cup!

Ted tripped on his shoelace,
I ran very fast,
Hurrah! I had won!
Poor Ted had come last!

Abigail Leslie (8)
Rupert House School

The Race

Oh how it was a long, long day
When the sun and wind had a race,
The sun was way behind, but,
Wind went at a steady pace.

The sun soon blinded poor old Wind
And he took a flying start,
Wind blew into a huge mountain
It tore poor Wind apart!

Wind pulled himself together
And returned into the race
He caught up on the sun
Soon he was in first place

Then Sun turned up the heat a notch
Poor Wind got far too hot
He thought he'd better have a rest
So Wind began to drop

Some clouds came and rained on him
And cooled him down quite soon
And so they both picked up again
Cheered on by the moon!

Sun began to set a bit
Wind overtook the sun
He flew straight past the finish line
Hip hip hooray, Wind won!

Olivia Morris-Soper (9)
Rupert House School

The Granny Race

'Twas the day of my birthday,
And Mum said to me,
'You will never guess
Whom we're going to see,
We're going to see Granny,
Take part in a race,
We hope that she'll win,
And take the first place.'

We went to see Granny,
Line up at the start,
She looked really good,
And keen to take part.

Then *boom,* the race started,
They started to run,
She seemed to be having,
A whole lot of fun!

Oh no, she's tripped over,
Fallen flat on her face!
She does not have a chance,
Of winning this race.

But yet she gets up,
And back on her feet,
Starts running again,
And soon wins her heat.

Now Gran's in the final,
She's doing quite well,
She's on her last lap,
And she hears the bell.

She gets faster and faster,
And puts on some speed,
She overtakes others,
And is now in the lead.

Jessica Ryan (9)
Rupert House School

The Horse Race

On the day of the race,
I jumped on my horse,
We went in the stalls,
At the start of the course.

The starter came up,
And off went the gun,
The gates opened wide,
The race had begun!

We galloped so fast,
We cleared the first jump,
I clung to the saddle,
Joe fell with a thump.

Next I galloped so fast,
I went at a great speed,
I passed all the others,
Into the lead!

I could then see the finish,
We'd ten metres to run,
I was first past the post,
I was so glad I had won!

Rebecca Roddan (9)
Rupert House School

The Monster That Ate The Universe!

There was a hungry monster that liked to eat all day
The kids got really nervous when they went out to play
They feared the monster would eat them if he came by their way
He'd already eaten Africa, said 'Goodbye' to Japan
'Farewell, New Zealand,' and 'Adieu, Amsterdam.'
The world was on his plate and the sea in his cup
There was no way to escape as he'd swallow us all up
The army tried to attack him and so did the marines
But this was the strongest monster the world had ever seen
And just when I thought it couldn't get much worse . . .

I
   saw
      the
         m
          o
          n
           s
            t
             e
            r
               eat
                 the
                   u
                    n
                     i
                      v
                       e
                        r
                         s
                          e!

Kate Radin (9)
Rupert House School

The Race

The wind fought through the rainforest,
And ripped two ancient trees,
And flung them to the leafy mud,
And sank them to their knees.

And as the trees lay fallen there,
Their seeds dropped to the ground,
They soon grew into saplings,
That spread new leaves around.

The saplings knew they had to race,
To the canopy so high,
The one that got there first would live,
And the other one would die!

In the canopy of trees,
There was a sunny hole,
Each had to get there first to live,
To reach there was their goal.

I decided I would name these trees,
The strong one I called, 'Greedy',
The other sapling was quite small,
And so I named him 'Weedy'.

Days went past and up they grew,
And Greedy grew quite tall,
While Weedy tried to catch him up,
I hoped he wouldn't fall!

Then Greedy started slowing down,
While Weedy took the lead,
The saplings grew together,
That had started from the seeds.

And together they both reached the top,
They spread their branches wide,
The race had ended in a draw,
They lived there side by side.

Georgia Chamberlain (8)
Rupert House School

The Daisy Chain Race

We are ready to make daisy chains
We really want to win!
The man will blow the whistle
And then we'll all begin!

We are trying to find daisies
And then we see a lot!
They are over in the corner
Growing in a pot!

The other team is trying
But we are still ahead
But then they see a hundred
In the flower bed!

We have grown our nails long
So we can make good holes
We thread them together
Our chains fill lots of bowls.

We are nearly finished
The time is nearly up
Our chain is the longest
We have won the Cup!

Chloë Winstanley (8)
Rupert House School

The Royal Race

The annual Tudor race starts again
It is for royals, both women and men
A gong has sounded, the race has begun.
The kings and queens begin to run.

Henry VIII is coming in last
He's so enormous he cannot run fast
Mary, Queen of Scots, has taken the lead
With her long legs she runs at great speed.

Elizabeth I runs the race well
Whether she'll win, no one can tell
Edward VI is going quite slow
But look at Mary I really go.

Catherine of Aragon's really quite fast
But little Jane Seymour's now rushing past
Henry VII beats Catherine Parr
The finishing line isn't that far.

Elizabeth of York has stopped to talk,
To Catherine Howard, Anne of Cleves walks
Into the lead comes Anne Boleyn
I'm sure that she is going to win!

Katie Adams (9)
Rupert House School

The Swimming Race

Gazing at the shimmering ripples,
Of the swimming pool with fear,
My heart is beating really fast,
The instructor is now here!

She holds the whistle in her mouth,
I shiver, full of fright,
A high-pitched shriek, I dive straight in,
And swim with all my might.

Everyone cheers at the side of the pool,
I probably will come last,
I am feeling embarrassed, I'll let my team down,
The others are going too fast!

I slice the water with my hands,
And kick my legs behind,
If I keep swimming, I could win,
These thoughts race through my mind.

I raise my head above the surface,
The others are metres away,
I know I can do it, this is my chance,
I'll win this race today!

The bright-coloured flags mark the finishing line,
The others have hardly begun,
I take a deep breath and dive underneath,
I can't believe it, I've won!

Emma Ford (10)
Rupert House School

The Race

We started the 800 metres race,
We had to go at a rather slow pace.

Bang! The race had started well,
But then the fastest runner fell!

When halfway round my first lap,
I really wanted to turn back.

Soon one whole lap was done,
But there were three more to run!

On my second lap I gasped,
All the rest were running fast!

On my third I went too slow,
There was still one more to go!

On my last I sped right up,
As I wanted to win the Cup!

To my delight I found I'd won
I was so glad that it was all done!

Sophie Frood (10)
Rupert House School

The Race

I was having a horse race today
I was so excited I shouted, 'Hooray!'
I went to the stables to get my horse
We got in the horse box and drove to the course
The whistle blew, we had to line up
We were racing to win the big Challenge Cup!
The gun went off, the horses began
I felt nervous as my horse ran.
Jessica and Lydia were cheering me on
My good friend, Lily, had already gone
Then her horse decided to chuck
Her off, that wasn't good luck!
Then Georgia arrived and started to cheer
I was quite nervous, the finish was near
After five minutes I found that I'd won
The big Challenge Cup! Oh, it was fun!

India Wishart (8)
Rupert House School

The Race

Maddy and Amy were having a race
On their ponies, Charlie and Tasha,
They were excited, they wanted to win
They felt they were under some pressure!

For the gymkhana they had to plait
Their ponies' manes and their tails.
They had to polish the saddle and bridle
And wash their hooves in some pails.

The got on their ponies and went into the school,
They trotted in and out of some cones
They got an apple out of a pail
They beat the strawberry roans!

Jess and Grace were cheering for Amy
While Laura was cheering for Maddy,
Amy was riding just in the lead
There were cheers from her mummy and daddy!

Lydia Tufnell (8)
Rupert House School

The Hair-Growing Race

'Mummy!' shouted Nathalia Waiters.
'I've found something in the papers.
You know I want to grow my hair?
Well, here's a competition where
You have to grow it really long
I want to win, I can't go wrong.

I'll go to the witch and get a potion,
Well make sure it's a hair-growing lotion.
Every night I'll put it on,
My hair will grow extremely long.
When the judge says who's won the race
I'm sure I'll be in first place!'

They went to the witch to get a potion,
She gave them her best hair-growing lotion.
Nathalia Waiters put some on,
Her hair started to grow super-long.
In an hour it had reached around
Her knees and then it touched the ground.

The next day when she woke up,
She knew she would win the Cup.
Because her hair was 12-feet long
She knew that she could not go wrong.
And of course, she won the race,
Rapunzel came in second place!

Katie Moberly (8)
Rupert House School

The Raindrop Race

One rainy day I sat in a car,
Hoping that we didn't have to go far,
I thought I should start to read my book,
But it wasn't there when I had a look!

So I looked out of the window to see what was there,
Two little raindrops fell from the air,
Another two fell on top of the car,
I named one Twinkle, the other one Star.

They trickled down as slow as a snail,
But suddenly it started to hail,
Star then suddenly went well ahead,
'Get a move on, Twinkle!' I said.

Star slowly came to a halt,
Twinkle shot off like a catapult,
Star sidled off to the right,
Dazzled by a car's headlight.

Then Twinkle met a squashed-up fly,
(There was no way he could get by),
He couldn't creep around the side,
Because the fly was squashed so wide,

The race was just about to end,
When the car went round a bend,
And Daddy turned the wipers on,
Twinkle and Star were suddenly gone!

Abigail McQuater (9)
Rupert House School

The Santa Race

Starting with a red woolly hat,
Each of the Santas look very fat.

They run up to the fake moustaches,
Let's see who can stick theirs on fastest.

They stick on snowy beards with glue,
Then they stick on eyebrows too.

Next the Santas stomp up to the trousers,
They pull the braces over their blouses.

They put on jackets of red suits,
And then they pull on big, black boots.

They race to buckle their belts on tight,
Their buttons shine in the gleaming light.

Then they jump into their sleigh,
They make their reindeer fly away!

Harriet Gardner (10)
Rupert House School

The Slayer

There was a sixteen-year-old name Buffy
She liked bunny rabbits that were fluffy
She slew all types of devils
But claimed not a medal
And got in a bit of a huffy!
One day not vamps but a god
Whilst slaying, met a guy called Tod
His real name was Riley
He looked at her slyly
This place smells worse than rotten cod!

Jodi Ferguson (10)
St John's Priory School, Banbury

The Secret Ballerina

I'm waiting to go on.
I'm nervous.
The lights are dim.
The curtains fly open and the music starts to flow
And I begin to dance like a doll on a music stand.

With graceful movements in a dainty pink tutu
I dance balletically, as light as a feather.

It's a magical night.
Everyone is staring at me.
I am the Prima Ballerina.
I am Cinderella
And I am dancing with Prince Charming,
With my fairy godmother watching over me.

I hold a pose.
I'm now flowing with the soft music playing.
My heart is thumping louder and louder
With every move I strike.

The dancing starts to fade.
The lights dim.
The music marches away
And my music box has now run out.

Everyone is throwing roses at my feet
And I am crying with joy.
Then a final pirouette . . .
And *crash!* I fall.
But I fall not from the stage
But from my bed to the floor.
It was all a dream
But oh, it was so beautiful while it lasted.

Perhaps I'll dance again tonight.

Georgia Leach (11)
St John's Priory School, Banbury

The Dundee Bee

There once was a man from Dundee
Who got very afraid of a bee
When he started to run
He got stung on his thumb
And took off as far as you could see.

Louis Harris (10)
St John's Priory School, Banbury

What More Can I Say?

As the music starts to play,
All the people begin to sway,
First fast and then slow,
It's taken over the whole row,
What more can I say?

They're playing my favourite song,
It doesn't go on for very long,
I really don't want to go,
Someone's calling me home,
What more can I say?

Rebecca Smith (10)
St John's Priory School, Banbury

Chocolate

C hocolate is my favourite
H ow can you disagree?
O range chocolate is my favourite
C reamy, and full of milk, I'm sure you will agree!
O pening a chocolate bar, the pleasure is supreme . . .
L ovely chocolates, soft centres and cream
A dore to eat it every night
T reat myself, what a delight
E very single night, every single night!

Thomas Callnon (10)
St John's Priory School, Banbury

Time

Time creeps on through night and day
In its strange and mysterious way
And we in our equally creative quay
Try to find its memory
We try and trap it in a clock and find out where it's been
The route it has taken through happiness and war
And when it walked through victory
And then when it saw loss
But we being the way we are
Will never ever catch it in our watch
For time is more powerful than water,
More powerful than wind
Time is one thing in a million things
And that is how it should be.

Imogen Webb (10)
St John's Priory School, Banbury

Puppy Eyes

My dog's eyes, they're really sweet
They look at you for a doggy treat
He looks and looks, his ears flat back
Then they perk up when he gets a snack.

My dog's eyes, they sparkle bright
Shining in the kitchen light
He barks all day, he barks all night
His eyes grow fierce and scrunch up tight.

My dog's eyes, can you resist
The way they stare, and twirl, and twist?
He's not a puppy, not anymore
But his eyes are still a puppy's, and them I adore.

Sophie Poole (10)
St John's Priory School, Banbury

A Cheetah's Triumph

He's a yellow killing machine.
In his eyes death roams free,
A movement to the left,
A movement to the right,
His eyes flicker, his ears tweak,
Something moves in the bush.

He's a yellow killing machine.
His prey is now in his view,
He springs towards the bush,
He chases towards the tree.
His prey, with fear in his eye,
Makes a quick dash for his life!

He's a yellow killing machine
Who creeps, sneaks and pounces.
His eyes of death are now content.
His lips, stained with blood, grin
As he returns to his young.
He's a yellow killing machine.

Harry Poole (10)
St John's Priory School, Banbury

The Lion

She roars all day and she roars all night,
Looking for something in her sight,
She pounces in the morning, evening too,
Looking for her food through and through.

Her cubs come running to look what she has got,
But they don't know that she has not.

Bang! Bang! The wild men shoot,
So cubs alone do not suit,
Got their mums for skins and rugs,
But the cubs just think they are thugs.

Elise Robinson (10)
St John's Priory School, Banbury

Be Frightened

As the Earth started to rumble,
I looked and could not believe my eyes,
As rocks began to tumble.
One night I looked up to the skies.

The volcano started to grumble,
And out came large, red rock,
I started running for my life,
As rock landed, block on block.

Everything was getting hotter,
And my heart was beating fast,
I ran and ran faster and faster,
Getting home to my family at last.

Then suddenly there came a big *boom!*
With people all around,
They were scared, frightened and dirty,
With no voices and no sound.

A loud bell was ringing in my ears,
I blinked my eyes to stare,
My mother stood there shaking me,
And said,
'You must have had a nightmare!'

Charlotte Ross (10)
St John's Priory School, Banbury

The Oil Painting

The patterns and swirls they live inside
The colours and splatters slowly glide
Everyone who stares at it too long
They will hear a long-lost song, lost song
'The oil painting's alive, alive
The oil painting's alive.'

All other artists will cry and weep
Picasso and Monet will think it's cheap
They're jealous and sad, so anxious, help,
When they have finished they'll loudly yelp
'The oil painting's alive, alive
The oil painting's alive.'

Sugary pinks and silver sparkles
Bright red streaks which make all eyes startled
People all like this picture so much
In its glass frame it wants to be touched
'The oil painting's alive, alive
The oil painting's alive.'

Octavia Homans (10)
St John's Priory School, Banbury

At The Seaside

When I'm at the seaside,
I love to play on the ocean edge,
And go on the pier and dive off the pier ledge.

Then I sit down on the golden sand,
And lie on my towel under the hot sun.

Time to go home from a long day,
A few nights go on and I think of the seaside,
Then soon I'll be going back.

Rachael Lever (8)
St John's Priory School, Banbury

Work

Work, work, I think it is bad
Sometimes it makes me very sad
My mummy says it is good for me
But I don't see why it should be.

Alicia Forsyth-Forrest (8)
St John's Priory School, Banbury

My Perfect Pets

Nippy is my hamster,
She is very, very sweet.
She, I am sure,
You would like to meet.

Fudge is my guinea pig,
He is very, very nice.
He always wrinkles his feet up,
When they touch the cold winter ice.

Penny is my goldfish,
She is very, very nutty.
She actually eats the corner off,
My mother's bacon butty.

Fluffy is my rabbit,
He is very, very silly.
He always chases my frog called Fred,
When he's sitting on his lily.

Freddy is my frog,
He is very, very cool.
He is actually quite nice,
When he's hopping around in his pool.

Libby Hart (9)
St John's Priory School, Banbury

Fire From Beneath

Fire is a tongue licking at you from the fireplace,
Like wild animals running all over the place.
It burns, it squirms and it quickly spreads,
Couldn't we use water instead?
Fire is death, makes me scared,
It is a tiger with its teeth bared.
Fire is a snake sliding around,
Bringing our trees down to the ground.
Fire is a massive rake,
Hoping for someone to make a mistake.
Fire is a very bad habit,
Its favourite meal is wood or cabbage.
How can we get rid of fire?
If only it would be a bit shyer.
Fire is a snake throttling its prey,
I'll make sure it goes away.

George Walker (10)
St John's Priory School, Banbury

Water Might Not Be What You Think

Water is a great big hand,
It grips the sand like glue,
It tumbles down into the earth,
Where no one knows what to do.

Water can be smooth,
Water can be rough,
Water can be fast,
Water can be loads of stuff.

Water can be rivers,
Water can be sea,
Water can be lakes,
Water can be rain.

Now do you think
Water is what it seems?

Hamish Preston (10)
St John's Priory School, Banbury

The Bull Train
(After seeing an old steam train and thinking of life)

Like a bull with speed.
The noise of its hooves thundering to the ground.
Its shriek of steam.
Its metal stomach on fire
And full or rage and anger.
Smoke bellowing from its large mouth.
It slows down and finally stops!

It roars to say, 'Hello'
To the other trains but they don't reply.
So it's mad now instead
Its boiling tummy now roars
And it's spitting all around
It's trying to say,
'I'm nice,'
Now it's saying . . .
'I am dangerous!'

Alexandre Dansette (10)
St John's Priory School, Banbury

My Friend

My friend is fun, she loves to play
she skips around and says, 'Hello,'
that is what she does.

My friend likes sleepovers
she thinks they're good fun
she has midnight feasts
and then in the morning she is full.

My friend gets sad when people die
she hugs me and even cries
but then she gets happy and doesn't cry.

Abbie Leach (8)
St John's Priory School, Banbury

At The Funfair

The lights that glow
all around,
and the Ferris wheel
going round and round.

Candyfloss, ice cream,
popcorn too,
and a bag of sweets
that I will share with you.

My favourite ride is
the merry-go-round,
it only costs
one pound.

There's not a place
I'd rather be,
than at the funfair
just you and me.

Sarah Williams (9)
St John's Priory School, Banbury

There's Not A Place I'd Rather Be . . .

There's not a place I'd rather be
than at home on the settee,
eating popcorn by the telly,
watching a movie, a friend and me.

There's not a place I'd rather be
than at the garage with my daddy,
watching him do lots of deals,
selling lots of big wheels.

There's not a place I'd rather be
than out shopping with my mummy,
spending lots of Daddy's money.

Hayley Wood (9)
St John's Priory School, Banbury

I Like

I like the sound of crashing waves,
I like the sound of birds,
I like the sound of people whispering,
It's true that I do.

I like the taste of ice creams,
I like the taste of chocolate,
I like the taste of sweets,
It's true that I do.

I like the smell of flowers,
I like the smell of babies,
I like the smell of ripe apples,
It's true that I do.

I like tastes and smells and sounds.

Vanessa Wilde (8)
St John's Priory School, Banbury

Water

Water can be blue,
murky or crystal-clear.
It can be rough or calm.
It can run down in streams
making a *beautiful* sound.

Imagine what it would be like
without water?

I would miss . . .
drinks, baths and water fights
soothing ice lollies and
hot water bottles.

Imagine
what it would be like
without *water!*

James Williams (8)
St John's Priory School, Banbury

Why?

Why, why do I cry
When everything goes her way?
Why, why do I lie
When people come to stay?
Why, why do I try
To keep the rules my way?
Why, why do I just want to cry?

Olivia Attley (8)
St John's Priory School, Banbury

There's Not A Place I'd Rather Be

There's not a place I'd rather be
than sitting by the crashing sea.
Eating ice cream on the sand
and watching all the seagulls land.
There's not a place I'd rather be
than sitting by the crashing sea.

There's not a place I'd rather be
than swinging on a swing, just me.
Just swinging in the sun
really can be a lot of fun.
There's not a place I'd rather be
than swinging on a swing, just me.

There's not a place I'd rather be
than at home with my family.
Reading books and writing too,
now that's what I like to do.
There's not a place I'd rather be
than at home with my family.

Isobel Green
St John's Priory School, Banbury

Animals At The Zoo

I love animals at the zoo
Big or small
Colourful or dull
Fast or slow
I love animals at the zoo
Fast-charging rhinos
Slow-moving turtles
Shiny-looking tigers
Dull-looking frogs
I love animals at the zoo.

Thomas Marsden (9)
St John's Priory School, Banbury

The Wendigo

The Wendigo is a slimy creature,
That is dreaded by most parents and teachers.

In the papers for the last few years,
There has only been one thing,
That has been described as clear:
'The Wendigo has struck again!'
It is written by famous reporters.
'Beware of the Wendigo,
It may strike again!'
If it does, you will soon find out,
It struck again on a Christmas Eve,
When a young boy the age of me
Was sitting under his verandah, happy
When suddenly the Wendigo came,
And frightened the living daylights out of him
His mum and dad watched, shocked,
As their son disappeared with one great gulp!

Sooraj Mahesh (8)
St John's Priory School, Banbury

Christmas Time

I love Christmas time
Eating Christmas cake
The excitement of opening presents
The smell of Christmas pudding baked.

I love Christmas time
Going out to play
In the cold snow
I just want to say.

I love Christmas time
Having snowball fights
Getting to sleep is very hard
As the cold creeps in the nights.

I love Christmas time
All the excitement and playing
All the opening and shouting
All the talk and saying.

I love Christmas time
All the presents and smells
The excitement of people
And pictures of bells.

I love Christmas time
Everybody happy at the end
Some going to sleep, some not
Time for family and friends.

I love Christmas time
Into bed now, all of us
In bed I listen to sounds
And I hear church bells.

Kara Watson (8)
St John's Priory School, Banbury

Water

The best thing
about being dirty
is getting clean
again.
Standing under
the shower,
feeling the warm
water on my
cold body.
The water cleans
my hair,
my face,
my knees
and my feet.
I look down and
see muddy water
doing down the
plughole.
I'm *so glad* that
I don't have to go
so far to get
water!

Fergus Preston (8)
St John's Priory School, Banbury

Water

Water is everywhere.
It's in tap, pump, well and river.
At sea, it's there again.
Sitting beside the swimming pool
it is so lovely and cool.
When you are looking at the sea
it sometimes turns into tea.
But! It's just silly water
playing tricks on you and me.

Daniel Norrell (9)
St John's Priory School, Banbury

Teeth

Some people have shiny teeth
Some have rotten teeth
Some have gold or silver teeth
I have a few gaps in mine!

Babies have no teeth at all
Children have milk teeth
Adults have big teeth
We all have to look after them all.

Fizzy drink will give you toothache
So will sweets and too much chocolate!
Cleaning your teeth twice a day
Will keep all the bugs and problems away!

Benjamin Hawkins (7)
St John's Priory School, Banbury

A Bird

A bird is strong.
It flaps its wings.
Floating through the air
With the whirling wind.
It dives into the sea
To catch a fish.
At night it settles
To go to sleep
Inside its fluffy feathers.

Sam Sorabjee (7)
St John's Priory School, Banbury

Water

Water can be rough,
Water can be blue,
Water can be grey,
Water can be dangerous,
Water can be calm,
Water can be almost anything!

Kyle White (8)
St John's Priory School, Banbury

Water Poem

We all need water to drink.
We are lucky it comes from a sink.
Others have to carry it from a well,
Which if not clean, can make you unwell.

Vanessa Polson (8)
St John's Priory School, Banbury

Water

Water is in the sea,
Water is for you and me.
I drink water every day,
I use water when I play.

    I love water,
    Do you love water?
    The sea has water that is fun.
    I love water warmed by the sun.

        I see water every day,
        I see water when I play.
        I drink water with my lunch,
        I have water with my brunch!

Elizabeth Hurst (8)
St John's Priory School, Banbury

The Sea

The sea is rough,
The sea is calm.
The sea can rumble,
Like a hungry bear.

The sea can have horses,
On the surface.
The sea can have hands
Rising higher and higher.

The sea creeps forward,
When it's hungry.
The sea goes back,
When it's full.

The sea stretches for miles,
The sea is very deep.
The sea sees everything,
In the light of the sun.

Akanksha Goyal (7)
St John's Priory School, Banbury

Water

I flow from spring to stream,
From waterfall to sea,
I hold the fish in my palm.
I carry the boats upon my shoulders,
I fall down your cheeks as tears.
I tumble down your face as snow.
I am angry as hail,
I am calm as mist,
I am everywhere!

Rhiannon Gray (8)
St John's Priory School, Banbury

Butterflies

Butterflies glittering in the sunlight, butterflies on the leaves.
Their glorious wings fluttering.
Their rich colours mixing in the air.
Butterflies, butterflies playing on the leaves.
Laying their eggs and eating leaves.
Those ugly caterpillars turn into very aesthetic butterflies.

Moronshayo Oshodi (8)
St John's Priory School, Banbury

Water

Water, water, rushing by
Everywhere about.
Rushing, rushing along the bank
As loud as a roaring plane.

Water can be peaceful
When it glides through woods,
And beautifully calm
When the wind is low.

Robert Tibbetts (7)
St John's Priory School, Banbury

Untitled

When the clean rain falls high from the sky
it makes muddy puddles.

When the sun shines bright,
the clear pond water gets warm,
you see ripples twinkle on top of the pond.

Oliver Walker-Savings (7)
St John's Priory School, Banbury

In My Pencil Case

In my pencil case there are,
The most weirdest things by far.

There's my pink, fluffy pen
And the one I borrowed way back when.

There's my chewed-up rule
Which I think is really cool.

There's hundreds of cartridges of ink
But I wish I could write in pink.

There is also my Biro
Which I bought in Cairo.

I can never find anything at all.

Poppy Hawkins (11)
St John's Priory School, Banbury

Animal Poem

A snake slithering through the sand
Like rope getting wriggled.

A dog happy in its kennel
Like a baby in its cot.

A monkey swinging on branches
Like a child playing in the park.

An ox in a muddy field
Like a boulder in the snow.

A cat on the sofa
Like a pillow on its bed.

Daniel Simpson (10)
Stanford In The Vale Primary School

Tiger's Eyes

Tiger, tiger in the night
Why do your eyes shine so bright?
As you walk here and there
I cannot help but to stop and stare
Like big orange suns in the night
Why do your eyes shine so bright?

Curtis Redman (10)
Stanford In The Vale Primary School

There Was A Man From China

There was a man from China
He was a very good mountain climber
He slipped on a rock
Split his sock
Now he is a whiner from China.

Max Johnson (11)
Stanford In The Vale Primary School

A Skidded Face

A skidded face,
A sad case.

A line wearer,
A car bearer.

A car carrier,
A metal barrier.

A code to make
Me road.

Craig Punfield (10)
Stanford In The Vale Primary School

Moose

A mythical creature standing on his lofty legs
The legendary beast.
Giant, colossal, standing high above the ground
Looking up at the towering beast is like looking up
At the tallest tower.

As he walks sturdily through the trees
Getting away from everything,
The historic creature looks through the trees and thinks,
Are these people afraid of me?
He runs and says, 'I am all of these things.'

Stephanie Jordan (10)
Stanford In The Vale Primary School

Warm And Cold

Puppy in the porch,
Like the shopping in the boot.
A caterpillar in a cocoon,
Like a bookworm in a book.

A dolphin dancing in the sea,
Like a hamster in a ball.
An otter in its bedding,
Like a batch of cookies in the oven.

A horse in the stables,
Like a person in a house.
A snow leopard running through trees,
Like people racing in a marathon.

Danielle Belcher (10)
Stanford In The Vale Primary School

Hear

At home I can hear:
TV singing to the theme tune of EastEnders,
Kettle bubbling as it boils the water,
Duvet rustling as people turn in their sleep,
Cat miaowing as it wants food
Can you?

At school I can hear:
Teacher shouting at someone being bad,
OHP humming to show children words,
Pen squeaking on board as Teacher writes our work,
Paper hissing as page turns in our book,
Can you?

On the street I can hear:
People's footsteps on the long, winding pavement,
Birds chirping tunes so sweet,
Lorries rumbling along the main road,
Trees waving in that lovely cool breeze.
Can you?

Lauren Pilcher (10)
Stanford In The Vale Primary School

Ocean Kenning Poem

A dolphin's dream
A seaweed green.

A crunchy crab,
A dolphin drag.

A sailing ship,
A dolphin dip.

A potion to make
me an . . . ocean.

Harriet Munday (10)
Stanford In The Vale Primary School

Animal Simile

A monkey swinging through the trees
Like a little boy on the monkey bars.
A dolphin crashing through the waves
Like a man jumping on a trampoline.
A robin sitting on the fencing hunting for food
Like a child waiting for its tea.
A tiger running to get some food
Like a sprinter in a hundred metre race.
A seal gliding over the sea
Like an aeroplane taking off.

Josh Satchell (11)
Stanford In The Vale Primary School

The Moose

The mighty ferocious moose stands proud.
The king of the forest, mysterious and unknown.
A massive historic creature.
His bulging eyes speak his feelings.
With his rugged fur and masculine horns.
His large head and tall body
Remind me of a giant.
Invincible.
Nothing stopping him in his path.
His sturdy gigantic body
Like a rock, stiff but still.

Amber Gifford (11)
Stanford In The Vale Primary School

My Animal Poem

Cheetah running through the jungle
Like a cat chasing a mouse.

Kitten dry in the outhouse
Like a snail in its shell.

Robin asleep in its nest
Like a cat by the fire.

Dolphin in the sea
Like a speedboat on the water.

Rachel Hanna (10)
Stanford In The Vale Primary School

Moose

The legendary beast wanders on,
Through trees and bushes,
Mythical in the thick mist,
Towering over me like a huge tree
Unbreakable solid figure.
Muscular body but shy like a child,
To me you are
Magical as a wand,
Wonderful as can be,
And I love *you!*

Gemma New (11)
Stanford In The Vale Primary School

The Blunder Dope Of The Woods

A beast
A legend
Its body so hulky and gigantic
His big, thick, fluffy, brown fur
His lanky, lofty legs
His rugged, round nose
His fantastic, white, huge antlers
The blunder dope of the woods.

Philip Johnson (11)
Stanford In The Vale Primary School

Eye Of An Owl

Shimmers of flame
A cold Christmas, starlit night
The lonely fox dreams

The black velvet night
The icy roads like thin glass
Ruins slice the sky

Roofs beneath the stars
Frost scattered in the darkness
The village, empty

A bright, crisp, still moon
Stumble on the dark town road
Wish for clear silence.

Rozanna Harrison (10)
Stanford In The Vale Primary School

Frozen Winter

A bright Christmas moon
A thin icicle shimmers
A still town - silence

A black velvet night
A dark street in a village
A lonely, cold lane

A fox on the roof
Asleep in a dream of bones
In the empty night

Stars light the darkness
Beneath the starlight
Lies a flame of hope.

Graham Edgecombe (11)
Stanford In The Vale Primary School

My Cat

A dog dreader
A cushion shredder

A fish eater
A hairy heater

A claw carrier
A mouse barrier

A catalogue to make me a cat.

Bill Fraser (10)
Stanford In The Vale Primary School

Cinquains

The Hot Holiday

Lazy
Hot holiday
Sunbathing on the beach
Eating a freezing cold ice cream
Lazy

The Spring Birth

Beauty
Babies are born
Flowers shoot up in spring
Greenery all around outside
Beauty

Christmas Spirit

Snowy
Cold Christmas frost
The frosty white Christmas
Family and friends at our house
Snowy.

Sherrie Drew (10)
Stanford In The Vale Primary School